Welcome
as a Way of Life

Welcome

as a

Way of Life

A Practical Theology
of Jean Vanier

Benjamin S. Wall

Foreword by
John Swinton

 CASCADE *Books* • Eugene, Oregon

WELCOME AS A WAY OF LIFE
A Practical Theology of Jean Vanier

Cascade Books
An Imprint of Wipf and Stock Publishers
199 W. 8th Ave., Suite 3
Eugene, OR 97401

www.wipfandstock.com

PAPERBACK ISBN: 978-1-4982-2568-7
HARDCOVER ISBN: 978-1-4982-2570-0
EBOOK ISBN: 978-1-4982-2569-4

Cataloguing-in-Publication data:

Wall, Benjamin S.

Welcome as a way of life : a practical theology of Jean Vanier / Benjamin S. Wall; foreword by John Swinton.

xx + 122 pp. ; 23 cm. Includes bibliographical references.

ISBN 978-1-4982-2568-7 (paperback) | ISBN 978-1-4982-2570-0 (hardback)) | ISBN 978-1-4982-2569-4 (ebook)

1. Vanier, Jean, 1928– 2. Developmentally disabled. 3. Hospitality. I. Title.

BV4461 .W40 2016

Manufactured in the U.S.A.   07/14/16

To Elisha Quinn, Genevieve Elise, and Cassian Alan,

Abide in love

Gianluca Baroncini was born in Bologna on December 20, 1968. He is a member of the L'Arche Bologna Italy.

> "This painting makes me happy. I was thinking about the friendship I have with Tiziana while painting. All those different materials, wax, wood, colors . . . are enjoining each other's company and presence, there is no solitude and isolation for the woman in the painting.

> In the L'Arche community in Bologna I feel well. I live this community. It is a place I like because of the people here, they are beautiful and they are nice with me. When I am here I feel inside myself a joy. Here I have a place where I can work. I take care of the garden and we have a lot to do with all the plants and the compost. Work is important for me.

> Jean Vanier had a good idea when he began living in L'Arche, he is a friend . . .

> to get to know our community you have to come and stay with us, to look to our paintings and eat pizza with us. We are happy to have guests and when I prepare the pizza I am glad to welcome guests to eat together . . . you are welcome in Bologna!"

*By how much the other may be least, so much
more does Christ come to thee through them*

—John Chrysostom, *In Act.* H. 45.3

*Great care and concern are to be shown in receiving
poor people and pilgrims, because in them more
particularly Christ is received*

—Rule of Benedict 53.15

Ubi caritas et amor, Deus ibi est

Where charity and love are, God is there

—Taize Hymn

Contents

Foreword

JEAN VANIER STANDS AT around six-and-a-half feet tall. The height of his body reflects the depths of his heart. In 1964 Vanier did a small thing. After spending time in Paris in various institutions for people with disabilities, he emerged shocked and determined to change things. His horror at the violence and oppression meted out to people with intellectual disabilities did not result in a political movement or a heroic act of social justice. Rather he did something very simple, but deeply radical. He took three men with severe intellectual disabilities into his home in Trosly-Breuil, northeast of Paris, and lived with them in community in the spirit of the friendships of Jesus and the teachings of the Beatitudes. On the first night one of the men, Dany, became so disturbed that he had to go back to the institution from which he had come. But Vanier and the two other men, Raphael Simi and Philippe Seux, persevered. They lived together not as carer and cared for, but as *friends* who shared their lives in mutuality and vulnerability. From that small gesture emerged the L'Arche (the Ark) movement, which now comprises 147 communities across the world, all of which live according to this powerful relational dynamic. But of course, like many stories that are tinged with romance, the reality is much more complicated.

There is no question that Vanier is a unique, wonderful, and in many ways saintly individual who sees the world differently from many others. His writings and his presence reveal a world of gentleness and humility; a world where the weak are considered strong and the vulnerable become paradigmatic of God's coming kingdom. Vanier, and the communities that he has founded, inspire and challenge us to think differently; to *be* different. I remember a few years ago meeting up with Jean at a get-together of the L'Arche theology group in Birmingham, United Kingdom. The meeting was held in a beautiful old nunnery on the outskirts of the town. I flew down from Aberdeen, jumped in a taxi and made my way to the venue. As I arrived and began to walk up the long driveway towards the nunnery, I saw Jean walking in the garden. When he saw me, his face lit up. I immediately felt welcomed. He began walking purposely towards me. When he was about six feet away he reached out his arms and offered me the possibility of an embrace. I moved forward and we entered into what was a quite wonderful non-self-conscious hug that was dripping with the nectar of communion. "John!" he exclaimed. "So good to see you. Let's walk." And so we walked hand-in-hand up the driveway towards the nunnery. Now, under normal circumstances I would feel rather strange about walking hand-in-hand with an elderly man in the garden of a nunnery! But that is not how it is with Jean. The grace of his presence overcame the power of my pointless self-consciousness and enabled a form of communion that simply would not normally have been available to me. Those of us who wish to hide behind barriers of self-consciousness, lack of humility, and a desire to please those who look at us even if we do not know them, find ourselves revealed in the presence of such embodied grace. On that day, Vanier's embrace functioned as an exemplar of the grace that the L'Arche communities have embodied and drawn to the attention of the world.

Vanier is special. Nevertheless, the standard narrative of the L'Arche communities can sometimes be construed in terms that are overly romantic. The very foundations of L'Arche were, as Benjamin Wall powerfully draws out, imbued with apparent failure. Dany was sent back to where he came from. Likewise the beautiful gracefulness of Vanier's life and presence is marked by the realization that in the face of the most vulnerable people Vanier could be tempted towards violence. Like all of God's creation, there is a shadow side to the story of L'Arche. In focusing on a deep and intricate practical theology of L'Arche's practices of welcoming, Benjamin Wall opens up the story of these communities in ways that are fresh, honest, and deeply significant for the communities and for the world that is the object of their signification. Benjamin Wall presents a picture of L'Arche that is deep and rich and honest. He holds in critical tension the beauty of community, the power of welcoming, and the dangers and difficulties that accompany such practices. As such, his contribution to our understanding of Jean Vanier and the L'Arche communities is both edgy and warm.

There are many accounts of the L'Arche communities that have been written over the years. Some of them focus on the nature of community, some narrate Vanier's life, some focus on the spirituality of the L'Arche communities and others emphasize his philosophy. There are however relatively few studies that have really tried to dig into the *theology* of Vanier and the deep and vital theological roots which formed and continue to sustain the L'Arche communities. Part of the reason for this is that Vanier is a rather strange theologian. As you read through his written works it is rare to find extensive referencing, complicated words and ideas, formal academic philosophy, or engagement with current debates around the epistemology or ontology of God. Instead, what one discovers are narratives, aphorisms, and nuggets of wisdom that reveal the beauty not only of disabled lives, but of all human lives. This could lead us to think that Vanier is the type of practical theologian who tends to have nothing to say to what we might call "formal academic theology." To think this would be a profound mistake, a mistake that Benjamin Wall is very aware of and seeks to address with care and sensitivity. Vanier's writing may appear to be simple, but once one begins to reflect theologically on what he says and what he does—and it is important to note that in Vanier's thinking there is no separation between the two—the depth of his theology quickly moves to the fore. As Wall theologically engages Vanier's thinking, so the richness and depth of Vanier's theology floats to the surface like cream on a fresh pint of milk.

The L'Arche communities are dynamic and ever changing. We need people like Benjamin Wall to help us track the changes and talk into to those complex and difficult issues that emerge when human beings attempt to live in community. I commend this book as a wonderful contribution not only to our understanding of Jean Vanier and the L'Arche communities, but more broadly to our understanding of humanness. Wall's work enables all of us in all of our different situations and contexts to discover a little bit more about what it means to be human and to live humanly in a world that often militates against both.

John Swinton

University of Aberdeen
September 2015

Preface

LIKE ALL THEOLOGICAL PURSUITS, this book is an attempt to furnish a theological reading of the practical impulses that inform and shape Jean Vanier's writings and the aims and social forming dynamics of L'Arche. One of the aims of this book is to develop a practical theological account of the role welcome plays in the shaping of the Christian ethos according to Vanier's communal account represented in his writings and exemplified within L'Arche. Throughout this book the writings of Jean Vanier are read within the frame of a theocentric account of ethics taking God to be the primary object of all ethical inquiry. Since Vanier's writings convey the notion that living fully human involves both an awareness and responsivity to God's activity in the world, the foregrounded contention of this book is that central to the tasks of Christian theology and ethics is listening to the Word of God. Vanier asks not how we ought to live but how our lives are to listen and remain responsive to God, and God appearing in and through God's Word, creation, and others in particular. Essentially, this work attempts to highlight how Vanier's writings and L'Arche theologically name what it means to be and become human rightly. To be and become human is to be addressed by God. As we will see, for Vanier, listening and responsivity to this divine address is central to the moral life of our creaturely existence.

Acknowledgements

THE FOLLOWING IS AN attempt to express with words my gratitude to the people whose counsel, reflections, assistance, encouragement, blessings, and prayers have made this book possible. At the top of the list is Brian Brock, Reader in Practical Theology at the University of Aberdeen, who assiduously encouraged me in the development of this work from its beginning to end. I am also indebted to the critical engagement of John Swinton, Chair in Divinity and Religious Studies at the University of Aberdeen, and Hans S. Reinders, Professor of Ethics and Mental Disability at the Free University of Amsterdam. Both men graciously served as conversation partners, providing substantive reflection and engagement during the earlier stages of this project.

I am also indebted to the Collegeville Institute for Ecumenical and Cultural Research at St. John's University in Collegeville MN for granting me time, space, and opportunity to engage the Brethren of Saint John's Abbey and the Sisters of the Order of Saint Benedict at Saint Benedict's Monastery; both monastic communities supported the early stages of the development of this book through their extraordinary Christian witness and hospitality, interactions, and conversations on Christian witness, hospitality, and friendship throughout the duration of my time in residence within the St. John's community. Additionally, I am extremely indebted to Sue Mosteller, who provided not only a wealth of wisdom and constructive feedback on my reading of L'Arche and Jean Vanier but also shared many experiences of her life in L'Arche in story form during our time together at the Collegeville Institute for Ecumenical and Cultural Research.

Acknowledgements

I am profoundly thankful to Jean Vanier and L'Arche Trosly-Breuil, who provided the opportunity for me to experience the beauty of genuine hospitality and gain a greater understanding of what so many people mean when they commonly characterize L'Arche as a prophetic witness in the world and Church. My time with Vanier combined with the numerous encounters with core members of L'Arche were far more life giving and resourceful than any publication and/or presentation I could find in their trove of resources. My brief time with Jean Vanier and L'Arche has had and continues to have a profound effect on my life and thinking about what it means to live and worship.

I am also very grateful to many colleagues in Houston Graduate School of Theology and Greensboro College. In particular, I am indebted to Douglas Kennard for reading and critiquing drafts of these chapters, Stephanie Hruzek for her encouragement and keen eyesight during final proofreading, and Robert Mclachlan, Cameron Moran, Cindy Burns, Emmanuel Paulpeter, Ashley Gibson, Fr. Carl Lund, Wesley Mclachlan, Rev. Alan Hawkins, and Dodd Drake for listening hearts, fruitful conversations, and spiritual nourishment during the final stages of this book. I am also thankful to Rosie and Anne Gant for their generous support of my post within the Religion, Ethics, and Philosophy department at Greensboro College.

Most importantly, my family has made all the difference. My wife Leah Elizabeth has been a vital resource for the development of this book. Thank you for your devotion, service, and love for Elisha Quinn, Genevieve Elise, Cassian Alan, and me. Thank you for the many wonderful conversations about our learning what it means to be and become human, what makes life together possible, and how to listen and remain responsive to God and God's ways within the story of our lives. I am also thankful for my children who faithfully welcome me home each day with joy and love. Your cuddles, hugs, and kisses are more than mere gestures of love; they are life-giving.

Benjamin S. Wall

Greensboro College
October 2015

Introduction

THIS BOOK IS ABOUT the practical theology of Jean Vanier. Drawing from the large corpus of Vanier's writings, this book situates Vanier's theological thinking on community, care, and what it means to be and become human in the context of "welcome." This book is an attempt to draw attention to how "welcome," for Vanier, entails a way of life visibly expressed through gestures of welcome rooted in love and trust that take shape in welcoming others, befriending the stranger, and celebrating difference; gestures that embody an ethos of counter witness predicated on a commonly held vision of the good life, a politics that refuses modern liberal societal tendencies to displace *being* and *belonging* subservient to *doing* and possession; gestures of genuine hospitality, mutual support, togetherness, and belonging that offer an alternative way of conceiving and naming the social forming dynamics within Christian community, with special attention given to how "welcome" occurs within the communities of L'Arche. Throughout this work I constructively develop and name Vanier's practical theology as a "theology of welcome," demonstrating how welcome underlies and informs Vanier's understanding and practice of a way of life embodied in listening and remaining responsive to God, and God's ways within the story of human existence in particular.

At a deeper level, this book assesses Vanier's thinking on the place and role both the self and community play in welcoming the truth of reality as it is revealed and given within community in order to prepare the way for exploring how "welcome," for Vanier, is a sign of community life, the concretization of individual and communal trust in God's providence, and a conduit of God's presence in the world. In order to demonstrate how welcome cultivates life and growth within community, one's life, and one's life in relation to the community, this book highlights how "welcome," for Vanier, is a way of life inclined toward listening and remaining responsive to others; namely, God who is wholly Other, and then to other people. Moreover, this work constructively examines how Vanier's thinking on community in connection with L'Arche's inability to welcome everyone provides an access point for understanding the ways in which weaknesses, boundaries, and limitations are not only inherent to community life but also one's true self.

In addition, this book surveys thematic aspects of Vanier's understanding of what constitutes humanity and the self, explores how his understanding of how becoming present to the dynamic of faith exemplifies the theological conviction that Christ's presence is realized within the ordinary composition of daily life, and identifies how his communal account of L'Arche raises conceptual questions about the values accorded to the self within our current contemporary forms of life. In doing so, this book examines how Christ's presence concretized in the other not only gives shape to what it means to be with and present-*for* others but also calls into question how human society has come to understand and behave toward conditions of human limitation. For this reason, an analysis of care provision within L'Arche, which is expressed throughout many of Vanier's writings, will be given in order to provide a lens by which we can better theologically distinguish what forms of care and treatment are humane from those that depersonalize and objectify persons.

Chapter one provides a brief sketch of the ethos of the age in which L'Arche emerged, characterizes L'Arche as the visible expression of Jean Vanier's faithful exploration of God's will, and outlines the significant stages in Vanier's life that have been instrumental in the shaping of his spiritual and intellectual development. Additionally, this chapter sets the stage for the examination of the impulses that underlie the development of Vanier's conceptual framework and accompany the concrete theological realism inherent in the lived contexts of community, care, and faith within L'Arche. Finally, this chapter summarizes the beginnings, growth, and structure of L'Arche in order to draw attention to how L'Arche exemplifies a renewed vision of peace for humanity.

Chapter two outlines central theological, ethical, and anthropological features that undergird and influence the characteristic spirit naturally to Jean Vanier's understanding of community. By foregrounding the distinctive attributes that characterize the communal ethos within Vanier's writings and L'Arche, this chapter develops a constructive theological-ethical account of listening in the shaping of the Christian ethos. Throughout this chapter, I explain how Vanier's understanding of community takes God to be the primary object of all ethical inquiry, conveys the notion that living humanly involves both an awareness and responsiveness to God's activity in the story of human existence, and calls attention to humanity's need to remain responsive to the God who appears in and through the other.

Chapter three identifies and describes how vulnerability underlies and informs Vanier's thinking on community and L'Arche. Throughout this chapter, I constructively explore how the weak and poor in society, according to Vanier, are visible expressions of the constant form of Christ's pneumatological presence within the world in order to highlight how vulnerable persons are sources of life, unity, and communion with God and others, and how communion with the weak and poor is communion with God in particular.

Chapter four consists of three parts. Part one analyzes how Vanier sees listening and remaining responsive to God's activity within the story of human existence as integral to what it means to be and become human. Part two examines how Vanier's communal account and practical theology of care provision within L'Arche raises conceptual questions about the values accorded to the self and the distinctive qualities that are often regarded as holding personhood, identity, and individuality in place within society. Part three provides a synopsis of Vanier's understanding of what roots community, what attitudes inform the ways of life in community, and what breaks down community in terms of what I propose to name as "faithful exploration" in remaining responsive to the presence of God within the course of life. By way of drawing attention to the emphasis Vanier places on God's ways with humanity in the course of life, the purpose of this final chapter of the book is to demonstrate how Vanier's account provides a platform for Christian ethics to explore ways of speaking about God.

In conclusion, Vanier and L'Arche offer a radical vision of the ways in which the specificity of Christ's claim on us is visibly expressed in and through welcoming the other. Taken as a synthetic whole, Vanier and L'Arche present a vision of Christian existence and witness that is prophetic in nature—to abide in love is to welcome others.

1

A Call to Welcome

THIS CHAPTER PROVIDES A brief overview of the beginnings of L'Arche, reads L'Arche as the visible expression of Jean Vanier's faithful response to and exploration of God's will, and outlines significant stages in Vanier's life that have been instrumental in the shaping of his spiritual and intellectual development. Along the way, this chapter analyzes the ways in which Aristotelian philosophy and ethics not only underlie the development of Vanier's conceptual framework but also influences and accompanies the concrete theological realism inherent in the lived contexts of community, care, and faith within L'Arche. Finally, this chapter draws attention to the inception, ethos, development, and organization of L'Arche in order to highlight the ways in which L'Arche epitomizes a radical vision of peace for humanity.

Jean Vanier and L'Arche

IN THE MIDST OF an era marked by global anxiety and international tensions forcing many societies, countries, and nation-states into competing modes of existence, Jean Vanier chose a course of action that would begin and continue to call into question the prevailing powers, principalities, and cultural undercurrents profoundly affecting the characteristic spirit of his time and future generations.[1] With determined efforts to reign in freedom, establish a just society, and nonviolently stand up to prevailing oppression, cruelty, and unreasonable repression of marginalized people groups, namely, "persons with intellectual disabilities," Vanier invited three men with intellectual disabilities (Raphaël, Philippe, and Dany) who had been living in a neighboring institution to live with him in a small house in Trosly, an old village in France (August 1964).[2] This was the beginning of the first L'Arche com-

1. This is not to deny the existence of positive occurrences in 1964. Yet, then prevailing Cold War and Vietnam War tensions, sudden and violent rebellions in Gabon, Brazil, and Laos, the Zanzibar Revolution, civil and ethnic riots in the United States, and the successful development of China's first atomic bomb, to name a few, characterized this distinct period of history.

2. Throughout his writings and reflections on living with persons with intellectual disabilities, Vanier makes a point to address how language evolves over time "according to culture, country and times." He writes, "People used to talk about the 'mentally retarded' or 'mental deficient'. Today we use other terms: 'people with learning disabilities' or people who are mentally challenged' . . . Behind the change of language is the desire to affirm that a person with a mental handicap is first and foremost a person, who should be respected and given the opportunity to exercise his or her particular gifts." Vanier, *Our Journey Home*, xvii. In this regard, I use the terminology "persons with disabilities" throughout this book. When citing Vanier and others I employ the terminology found within the original context of those references. Additionally, it should be noted that even though these characterizations go against

munity.[3] Yet, L'Arche was no ordinary, sudden, or serendipitous undertaking. Instead, it was and is the embodiment of Vanier and others' faithful exploration of God's will involving a life of learning how to listen and remain responsive to God's activity in the story of human existence. Though originating out of a personal response to God's call upon Vanier's life, L'Arche, from the beginning, included encountering others. Encounter is an important theme throughout Vanier's writings and reflections on community. Reflecting on the entailments pertaining to and flowing from encountering others in community, Vanier explains that the cultivation and growth of trust stems from living together, especially when we live with others in ways that affirm the fulfillment of others' lives; gestures that occur in and through listening to who they are.[4] On this account, listening cultivates trust and genuine meeting, encounters that give way to the lowering and breaking down of defense mechanisms related to who we are. By way of a gradual relationship in the encounter, the meeting, and through listening, others become conscious of their importance and value; they discover who they actually are. Living with people who are broken, according to Vanier, helps them to perceive exactly their value and that they have something to give.[5] Correspondingly, "to talk about the encounter one should speak about the encounter between mother and child, which is essentially a celebration. Here, trust is born. The child knows she is loved and that she is seen as

certain cultural assumptions that see "weakness" as a defect and desire everyone to be strong and autonomous, when appropriate I follow Vanier and refer to "persons with disabilities" as well as persons who are in need of care as "poor," "weak," and "the least of these."

3. For a more detailed account of the common particulars of the beginnings of L'Arche see Whitney-Brown, *Jean Vanier*. Cf. Spink, *The Miracle, the Message, the Story*.

4. Jean Vanier (Founder of L'Arche) in discussion with the author, September 27, 2011. Here I am summarizing a personal interview I had with Jean Vanier at L'Arche in Trosly-Breuil, France in 2011.

5. Vanier, discussion. See Vanier, *The Challenge of L'Arche*; and Vanier, *Our Journey Home*. For secondary sources on these particulars see Cerac, "The Poor at the Heart of Our Communities," 25–35; and Reinders, *Receiving the Gift of Friendship*, 335–40.

precious. She is not just listened to through the ears, but listened to through the body. True encounter gives way to true hospitality. Since the word *hospitality* entails taking people into oneself, the encounter is a way toward communion."[6] For Vanier, "mutuality," "trust," "listening," "celebrating," and "meeting" reveal what occurs in the linking between listening and encounter; "meeting," "encounter," and "trust" all relate to and deal with listening.[7]

Living and being with others are integral to the commonly held vision in which belonging and communion with others is visibly expressed in being present-*for* the other within L'Arche, particularly in and through the economy of caring, a way of life therein. Vanier's emphasis on belonging and communion is often expressed in terms of "being with" others as a way to articulate the ways in which love is concretized within L'Arche. Love requires more than doing things for others. It involves being with others and takes shape in and through the process of becoming friends, a process that demands dynamic relational gestures such as presence, welcome, listening, and mutual willingness to be vulnerable, to name a few.[8] Correspondingly, being with others characterizes the nature, scope, and aim of the type of care provision within L'Arche exchanged between carers and those to/for whom care is rendered. At this point it is important to note that being present-*for* others in need of care is not the same as doing things for persons in need of care. Rather, being present-*for* the other involves attitudes and expressions analogous to the relational characteristics Vanier highlights above. John O'Regan writes:

> It is so easy to be present with another; this is simply a matter of physical nearness and connotes nothing whatever of friendship. Indeed one can have this sort of closeness with an enemy! It takes little besides ingenuity to be present to another in the sense of wanting to get all I can from him . . . There is no percentage in the present-for partnership; it is that benevolent friendship of Aquinas

6. Ibid.

7. Vanier, discussion.

8. Vanier, "L'Arche—A Place of Communion and Pain," 16–17.

that seeks the good of the other as its primary purpose.
It is real agape, a covenant-like love that has its eye on
nothing, but its heart and whole energy devoted to the
good and growth of the other.[9]

Commenting on relational dynamics of presence, Vanier writes,
"To be present to the despised, the poor, and the rejected, L'Arche
needs to move from a vision of power, even the power to do good,
to receiving the Paraclete, the Spirit of Truth promised by Jesus so
that we all grow in love *for* each person and particularly the most
despised."[10] On this account, being present-*for* the other entails
more than a mere presence and/or nearness with and/or to others; it involves a real covenant-like love, friendship, and devotion,
which holds the capacity to guard against artificial and pretentious
relationships.

In the contexts of community, caring, and being with others,
being present-*for* the other is not a mean toward an end—virtue
and character development and/or moral formation—as if those
persons who seek to be present-*for* others are seeking to fulfill
an ethical imperative in an attempt to be morally formed. As we
will see, the self, according to Vanier, receives its ethical form in
relation to the other via being present-*for* others in faithful listening and remaining responsive to the presence of God within the
story of human existence. Moreover, being present-*for* the other
is not read from the perspective of a unilateral dynamic of human agency—self-determined efforts of exclusively doing things
for others. Though doing things for others is a necessary part of
caring practice that occurs within L'Arche, gestures of doing are
carried out in light of a commonly held vision of the good of the
other that underlies, informs, and shapes gestures of belonging
and being with others.

Correspondingly, being present-*for* the other in the context
of care provision within L'Arche does not entail a type or set of caring practices designed to reveal the value or worth of others lives.
In other words, caring for the other does not constitute the worth

9. O'Regan, "Listening."

10. Vanier, *An Ark for the Poor*, 17. Italics mine.

of another life. Rather, being present-*for*, read from a theocentric perspective, affirms the inherent worth and value of others' lives. Moreover, it is the commonly held vision, goods, and politics related to the intrinsic worth and incomparable value of all persons that ultimately serves as the basis of community, covenant-like friendship, and a sharing of life with others; a commonly held vision concretized in being present-*for* others. I will return to these particulars in chapter 3 in relation to what I see as Jean Vanier's emphasis on the significance of being present and caring for each other and for each other's growth in understanding what makes community possible as an indispensible constituent of L'Arche.[11]

Being present-*for* another is a form of self-expression that calls the foregoing distinctive attributes belonging to the characteristic spirit of the age into question. By way of being present-*for* the other one subserviently assumes a position of lesser importance in which true self-actuality is constituted in belonging to, communion with, and responsiveness to others. What is being implied here is that communion with, belonging to, and being present-*for* the other precedes doing *for* others. In being with and present-*for* others, one abandons the propensity toward self-preservation, dominance, efficiency, competition, and pleasure while simultaneously offering a counter-witness against forms of self-projection in which the self is pretentiously bestowed and/or forced upon the other. As we will see, one's faith in the concrete reality that the other lays claims to one's being, leads to the discovery of the meaning of faith in practical life in relation to others' being—a discovery of ways in which others' being is placed before possession and/or possessiveness. Hence, the self receives its form in relation to the other. Being present-*for* another is at the heart of Vanier's theology and the ethos of L'Arche.

Within L'Arche, it is in living and being with and present-*for* others that persons—carers and cared for—come to perceive the value of each other and one's true self. On this account, the discovery of one's inherent worth and true self is not a phenomenon exclusive to persons with disabilities as if they are solely in need of

11. Vanier, *Community and Growth*, 20.

discovering their true inherent value. A key point to Vanier's writing and L'Arche is the significance of the attempt to understand our own vulnerability in order to discover the inherent worth of our true self, given constraints. As we will see, Vanier believes that when persons learn to welcome reality as it is revealed and given, which entails the reality of one's own vulnerability and brokenness, they learn to welcome oneself in truth.

Aristotle in the shaping of Vanier's conceptual development and L'Arche

Prior to the first L'Arche community Vanier spent eight years (1942–1950) as a naval officer in both the British and Canadian Navy. Throughout his military career Vanier became extremely conscious of a world full of devastation in which hope, forgiveness, human solidarity, and peace were scarce. He writes, "[These] years were taken up in a world of efficiency, controlling, and commanding others. I was a technician of destruction."[12] After a few years, Vanier began to reflect on questions concerning the meaning of life, his Christian faith, and Jesus' message of peace and vision for humanity, leading him to depart from the navy.[13] He recounts, "I felt called by Jesus to take another path, the path of peace."[14] After departing from the military Vanier spent many years under the tutelage and spiritual direction of Thomas Philippe, a Dominican priest and professor of theology and philosophy (1950–64), earned his doctorate in the area of Aristotelian philosophy (1962), and took a permanent professorship position at St. Michael's College in Toronto (1963-64). During this time Vanier's study of Aristotelian philosophy and long time friendship with Père Thomas provided intellectual and spiritual foundations that continue to influence and shape his life, writings, and work in L'Arche.

12. Vanier, *From Brokenness to Community*, 11.

13. Vanier, *Made for Happiness*, xii.

14. Vanier, *From Brokenness to Community*, 11.

During his doctoral studies Vanier devoted his time and attention to acquiring knowledge on Aristotelian philosophy and ethics. In 1962 he defended his doctoral thesis *Happiness as Principle and End in Aristotelian Ethics* at the Catholic Institute in Paris.[15] Even though Aristotle does not appear as a prevalent figure in Vanier's writings after the early 1970's, other than in his republished doctoral thesis, Vanier's conceptual Aristotelian beginnings have continued to influence and inform his writings and work in L'Arche.[16] Jacques Dufresne writes:

> In the wake of Aristotle, he [Vanier] also knew how to avoid another trap, that of the idea of a dualism of body and spirit. To listen to people, to touch reality—first, the body—this is his primary concern. The substantial union of the spirit and body is at the heart of the notion of human beings for Aristotle and St. Thomas Aquinas. Given how much incarnation means to him, Jean Vanier could not but adhere, without reservation, to such ideas as this one: "There is nothing in the mind that has not previously passed through the senses." He further insists on the importance of the senses to the point of speaking of the body as if it includes the soul.[17]

Throughout his thesis Vanier analyzes how Aristotle's view of ethics and happiness provide access to understanding the meaning of creaturely existence. Vanier places ethics within a positive register when interpreting the Aristotelian philosophical foundations of moral science. He writes, "Ethics help us to clarify what is a truly human act, what justice is and what the best activities are—those that render us more human and happiest. They help us better understand to what our freedom is calling us."[18] For Vanier, ethics provides clarity into our most profound inclinations with the intention to bring them to their ultimate fulfillment. Vanier

15. Vanier, *Made for Happiness*, xii-xiii.

16. Vanier's doctoral thesis has been recently republished under two titles: *Made for Happiness: Discovering the Meaning of Life with Aristotle*, and *Happiness: A Guide to a Good Life, Aristotle for the New Century*.

17. Dufresne, "A Road to Freedom," para. 10.

18. Vanier, *Made for Happiness*, xiii.

understands Aristotle's ethics originating from the experience of desired ends that attract humans toward genuine happiness and fullness of life.[19] Vanier's understanding of happiness is characteristically Aristotelian; it is analogous to Aristotle's *eudaimonia*, happiness as human flourishing. This account presupposes that every man and woman inherently possesses the desire to experience genuine happiness originating from fulfilling activity that enables humans to reach their full potential, to become accomplished, and to attain full maturity. On this account, Vanier perceives Aristotle's intended meaning of ethics as moving beyond the sphere of abstraction. He writes, "Aristotle's ethics are not therefore based on an idea but on the desire for fullness of life inscribed in every human being . . . [They] require that we work on ourselves."[20]

Vanier's account of Aristotelian ethics calls attention to the relationship between moral science and anthropology. Vanier describes Aristotle's ethics as "an actual moral science: the science of man."[21] As we will see, this linkage is vital for understanding particulars undergirding Vanier's theological anthropology. On this account, Aristotelian ethics engenders existential questions on the meaning of life and provide access to understanding what actions best embody what it means to be fully human. Consequently, reaching one's full potential, becoming fully accomplished, and attaining full maturity, or more precisely, "being fully human" does not mean simply obeying laws that come from outside.[22] Therefore, ethics involve more than established rules of conduct and appeals to unconditional moral maxims that are perceived as binding in each and every circumstance and independent from individual motives and/or dispositions. Vanier writes:

> If we do not become fully accomplished, something is lost to the whole of humanity. For Aristotle this accomplishment derives from the exercise of the most perfect activity: that of seeking the truth in all things, shunning

19. Ibid., x–xi.
20. Ibid.
21. Ibid., 2.
22. Ibid., 7.

lies and illusion, acting in accordance with justice, transcending oneself to act for the good of others in society . . . Law does not necessarily have any impact on the most profound driving forces of our action.[23]

Necessarily, an ethics of law does not determine what follows.[24] Instead, it is an ethics of desire in which the subject who acts experiences the inclination that moves them consciously toward desired end(s). Accordingly, an ethics of desire, for Vanier, names the nature, scope, and meaning of Aristotle's moral science—"that attraction which makes us rush towards what we perceive to be the good" for ourselves and the good of society.[25] Commenting on Aristotle's use of *orexis,* desire, Vanier writes, "*Orexis* . . . is a generic term that encompasses not only the passions but also the will or "rational appetite" . . . Experience might suggest the impulses of passion are not the same as those of will. But Aristotle uses the single generic word *orexis,* to designate [this] attraction . . ."[26]

According to Vanier, Aristotle draws attention to the need to thoughtfully consider what it is that attracts humans toward desired ends. Therefore, ethics presuppose listening and responsiveness to the self and its relation to desired goods. Vanier states, "According to Aristotle, to adopt an ethical approach thus supposes that we set about listening to what it is that profoundly attracts us and that we familiarize ourselves with the kind of vision that sees things as moving in conformity with desire. This, far more than any sense of law, is the ethical person's prime virtue."[27] Clearly, Vanier believes every man and woman inherently possesses both the desire to experience happiness and ability to consciously listen and remain responsive to the goods that attract us toward the ends we desire. Yet, this does not ensure that every man and woman will desire to act upon natural inclination(s) they possess and/or possess the wisdom to seek truth in all things, evade the illusory,

23. Ibid., xiv, 7.
24. Ibid., 6.
25. Ibid.
26. Ibid.
27. Ibid.

act in conformity with justice, and transcend oneself to act for the good of others in society. Aware of these dilemmas, Vanier appeals to what he perceives as Aristotelian realism that presupposes the need for distinguishing and choosing between what is truth from falsehood. Vanier writes, "If we are to remain on course, the ethics of desire must be combined with a sense of discernment and choice."[28] Hence, discernment and choice give definite form to listening and responsiveness in the shaping of Aristotelian ethics. As we will see in subsequent sections, "listening," for Vanier, plays a vital role in the shaping of his ethics, theological anthropology, and work within L'Arche. Though he retains the Aristotelian notion of discernment and choice in connection with listening to the inner depths of ourselves in order to distinguish desires that are superficial from those that are more profound, Vanier throws these Aristotelian sensibilities into a different key of welcoming and accepting that which is true according to the reality of one's self, as it is given and revealed— reality as it *is*—read from a theocentric christological perspective associated with divine providence.[29] For this reason, it is my contention that Vanier, though retaining the "object" of listening from Aristotle's account here, further develops it by way of situating both the "object" of listening and "listening" within a theological register on welcoming reality as the concretization of one's trust in God's providence.

Vanier places "becoming fully human" within an active register involving individuals reaching their full potential, becoming fully accomplished as possible, attaining full maturity, and discovering how to orient their life in the best possible direction. Although this ethical approach appears individualistic it does not necessarily confine one to such a view. Vanier writes, "At the very beginning of *Ethics*, Aristotle states that this science is subordinate to political science, because it is nobler to act in order that a large

---

28. Ibid., 7.

29. Throughout this book I italicize *is* in the context of "reality" in order to lay stress on how reality in relation to the "self" involves things as they actually exist, as a way to juxtapose a false idea of what one might think and believe concerning one's "self."

number may attain happiness than to act only for one's own sake."[30] Thus, reaching one's full potential, becoming fully accomplished as possible, and attaining full maturity are subordinate ends oriented toward a political dimension that integrates both civic and social spheres of life in which one lives out one's full humanity for the good of others in society. Discovering how to orient one's life in the best possible direction, for Vanier, presupposes acknowledgment and affirmation of the other's existence. Commenting on these particulars within *Nichomachean Ethics*, Vanier writes, "In a broader sense, happiness has a social and civic dimension. The man who wishes to be fully human cannot remain a stranger to city life."[31] The essential point that Vanier insistently affirms here and in other writings is that becoming fully human not only involves fullness of life but ultimately takes shape by way of living for the good of others in society. For Vanier, attuning oneself in relation to others and their good makes being and becoming fully human possible.

Undoubtedly, the foregoing particulars relating to Aristotelian thought play a vital role constituting Vanier's intellectual foundation and continue to influence and shape his life, writings, theology, and work in L'Arche.[32] Vanier writes, "[Aristotle's] thinking spans the centuries and is still relevant to us today."[33] Influenced by Aristotle's thinking on the good of others in society, Vanier's writings focus on the meaning of life and aim to provide access to understanding what it means to be fully human. Correspondingly, his writings seek to enable others to reach their full potential, to become accomplished, to attain full maturity, or more precisely, "to become fully human."[34] On the whole, Aristotelian thinking

30. Ibid., 163.

31. Ibid., xii. See Aristotle, *Nichomachean Ethics*, 1155a.

32. In keeping with the scope of this book, the following is in no way an exhaustive account of the innumerous ways Aristotelian thought corresponds to and influences Vanier.

33. Ibid., x. For a more detailed account of the relevancy of Aristotelian thinking within Vanier's work see *Made for Happiness*, 179–98.

34. For accounts in which these anthropological particulars are found see Vanier, *Becoming Human*; Vanier, *Man and Woman God Made Them*; Vanier,

has an atmospheric impact rather than being directly incorporated into Vanier's thought. It sets certain intellectual trajectories and offers core beliefs that underlie Vanier's writings. To a similar degree, many of his writings possesses qualities and features in common with Aristotelian appeal for the organization of a just society in which all members are enabled to become fully accomplished and live well within it.

Although comparable in certain respects, the corresponding particulars between Aristotle and Vanier's thinking within the foregoing analysis are not inherently homologous in every detail. Vanier broadens Aristotelian thinking concerning *logos*, calls into question hierarchal divisions between persons, and exposes many other Aristotelian shortcomings.[35] Rather than affirming that it is the *logos* in relation to value placed on rationality and intellectual capacity alone that constitutes what it means to be human, thus making a greater or lesser degree of autonomy possible and/or drawing individuals closer to God, Vanier affirms that "every human being, regardless of his or her [rational or intellectual] limitations, culture, or religion, is important and valuable and should be respected."[36] Vanier writes, "The worst ill is disdain of another person, which can lead to oppression and the suppression of human life. In order to progress towards the fullness of life that is inscribed in his or her being, every person, at some time or other, needs others."[37] Correspondingly, Vanier's writings draw attention to society's need for celebrating difference, encountering the other, and welcoming the otherness of the other. Though he favors the Aristotelian impulse of friendship being an essential part of human life, Vanier strongly critiques Aristotle for his ignorance on the value of an encounter between the rich and the poor, men and

---

Our Journey Home.

35. For a detailed account of the shortcomings and the value of Aristotelian ethics in Vanier's writings see *Made for Happiness*, 179–98.

36. Ibid., 180–85.

37. Ibid.

women, or more precisely, between unequals that moves beyond a mercantilistic perspective.[38]

Additionally, Vanier calls into question Aristotelian sensibilities concerning happiness consisting in relation to achieving the greatest possible autonomy. He contends, happiness consists of "a sharing of hearts and humility in relation to others," emerging from a *communion* "that is the sharing not merely of great and fine activities, beautiful thoughts, and generosity, but also of their shortcomings, their weaknesses, and their affective needs."[39] Flowing from his "experience of life among fragile women and men wounded by illness and rejection," Vanier extends justice to persons with disabilities, integrates Christian theological particulars with his ethical and anthropological thinking, and repeatedly articulates how L'Arche is rooted within and profoundly affected by the Christian theological tradition.[40] What is being implied here is that Vanier's intellectual development, though heavily influenced by Aristotle's philosophical and ethical thinking on humanity and the good, is not one of unbroken continuity with his Aristotelian beginnings. In other words, Vanier's basic conceptual framework is not simply applied Aristotle. Instead, it has developed over time in the course of his life in experience. Commenting on the ways in which his studies in Aristotle assisted him with ordering his thoughts and helping him to distinguish what really matters from what is less important, Vanier writes, "Aristotle loved all that is human. He made me pay attention not primarily to ideas but to the reality and experience."[41] Therefore, Aristotelian thought was a catalyst for listening and remaining responsive to the present moment. Attending to the present moment within the course of his life at L'Arche "has been, and is, a profound experience . . . both humanly and spiritually."[42] As a result, people with disabilities,

38. Ibid., 185.
39. Ibid.
40. Ibid., xiv.
41. Vanier, *Our Journey Home*, xv.
42. Ibid., xiv.

Vanier explains, "have taught me much about human nature and the real meaning of human existence."[43] He continues:

> They have taught me more about the gospel and even about human relations than all the great psychological and philosophical concepts; or rather they have allowed me to catch a glimpse of what should be true theology, true philosophy and true psychology. More than this, I have discovered Jesus in them, Jesus radiating goodness, Jesus the mirror of purity, Jesus meek and humble, and sometimes Jesus suffering and in agony . . . truly strength lies in weakness.[44]

Christian Spirituality in the Shaping of Vanier & L'Arche

Christian spirituality plays both a necessary and profound role in the shaping of Vanier's life and writings and the emergence of L'Arche. Vanier writes, "Spirituality is like a breath of inspiration that strengthens our motivation . . . [It] helps us better understand to what our freedom is calling us."[45] Throughout his writings Vanier emphasizes how spirituality, or more precisely, his Christian faith and the spiritual guidance of Père Thomas, helped him discern God's call on his life to a path of peace.[46] In response to this call—originating in Jesus' life, message, and vision for humanity—Vanier gave up his naval career to search for the meaning of life in his Christian faith, learning to trust God as he continued to discern God's divine vocation for his life.[47] Departing from the navy (1950) Vanier entered a time of intellectual and spiritual tutelage under the guidance of Père Thomas at Eau Vive and began working toward his doctorate. In a 2005 interview Vanier reflects,

---

43. Vanier, *Eruption to Hope*, 39.

44. Ibid., 46.

45. Vanier, *Made for Happiness*, xiii.

46. Vanier, *From Brokenness to Community*, 11.

47. Whitney-Brown, *Jean Vanier*, 24.

"Père Thomas didn't give answers. He provided tools for people to recognize and understand the choices in their lives. [He] would listen and then say, 'Pray about it.' [He] helped me to discover the Holy Spirit within me. His was a pedagogy of helping people to trust themselves to trust God."[48] In the light of the foregoing analysis on Aristotelian thought in the shaping of Vanier's conceptual framework, it is important to note the correspondence between Vanier's reflection on the type of spiritual tutelage he received from Père Thomas—"[he] helped me to discover the Holy Spirit within me"—and the Aristotelian call to listen to one's own desire in the light of the nature each person has received, recognizing and respecting the place in which nature has placed each person. However, offering a full-scale account on whether or not this pneumatological reflection is a full-on baptizing of this Aristotelian sensibility lies beyond the scope of this book. During this contemplative period Vanier gave frequent time and attention to cultivating both his intellect and spirituality. Carolyn Whitney-Brown, a member of the L'Arche Daybreak community in Canada from 1990 to 1997, writes, "Vanier threw himself into his studies, the manual work of the community, and direction, both intellectual and spiritual, from Père Thomas."[49]

Throughout this time many circumstances relating to the structural arrangements of Eau Vive as well as relations between Père Thomas and Rome and Vanier occurred resulting in the removal of Père Thomas from Eau Vive and Vanier's appointment to assume its leadership.[50] Shortly thereafter Rome and others would begin to vet for and anticipate Vanier's priestly ordination. Nevertheless, Vanier discerned that the path of peace to which he was initially called lay outside ecclesiastical structures.[51]

In response to his spiritual intuition Vanier departed from Eau Vive to continue completing his doctorate. Shortly after completing his degree Vanier was hired to teach philosophy at

48. Ibid. See Vanier, *Made for Happiness*, 189, 193.

49. Whitney-Brown, *Jean Vanier*, 24.

50. Ibid., 24–25.

51. Ibid., 25.

St. Michael's College in Canada. Before starting his professorship (1964) Vanier spent time in Trosly France helping Père Thomas move and transition into his new chaplaincy at Val Fleuri, an institution for men with intellectual disabilities. During his stay Vanier encountered first-hand society's exclusion of persons with disabilities. In the midst of deplorable realities originating from institutionalized life and the collective cacophonous voice of those he encountered at Val Fleuri, Vanier began to realize that any idea of peace was absurd in a society characterized by an ethos of denying and disparaging persons.[52] Reflecting on the invariable voice of those he encountered during his visit, Vanier writes, "Each of them starved of friendship and affection; each one clung to me, asking, through words and gestures: 'Do you love me? Do you want to be my friend?' . . . 'Why? Why am I like this? Why do my parents not want me? Why can't I be like my brothers and sisters who are married?'"[53] Accompanying these cries of utter rejection were long histories marked by rejection and intense suffering at the hands of parents, individuals, institutions, asylums, and/or society as a whole. "All this completely changed my life," Vanier writes.[54] If an ethos of exclusion prevailed upon individuals, institutions, and society, then peace, for Vanier, not only seemed absurd but absolutely impossible. Commenting on the circumstances that brought him into contact with persons with intellectual disabilities, Vanier writes, "I discovered how divided and fragmented our societies are . . . I realized peace could not prevail while no attempt was being made to span the gulf separating different cultures, different religions, and even different individuals."[55] Though not immediately or fully known at the time, Vanier's initial call from God to a path of peace was developing into something more concrete.

Before leaving to return and take up his teaching post at St. Michael's Vanier was confronted with the allure of Père Thomas's

---

52. Vanier, *Our Journey Home*, vii. See Vanier, *From Brokenness to Community*, 15; Vanier, *Encountering 'the Other*,' 17.

53. Vanier, *Our Journey Home*, vii.

54. Ibid., viii.

55. Ibid., xiii.

calling him to do something with persons with disabilities.[56] And it was during his first term at St. Michael's that Vanier begin to discern the concrete form his call from God would take. At the close of his first teaching term Vanier moved to France, bought a small dilapidated house in Trosly, and invited Raphaël, Philippe, and Dany, three men with disabilities, to live with him.[57] This was the first L'Arche community.

Originating in a call from God—rooted in the gospel of Jesus Christ—both Vanier's life and L'Arche embody a path of peace extending beyond conceptual limits of abstraction. Each of these particulars witness to God's activity in the story of human existence and convey the notion that living fully human presupposes an awareness of and responsiveness to God's divine movement in the world. Consequently, Vanier's life and writings and L'Arche explicitly call attention to both individual's and society's need to remain responsive to the other, especially persons who are weak, marginalized, and poor. These particulars challenge modern ethical thinking in so far as they ask not how we ought to live but how our lives are to remain responsive to God and God appearing in and through the other, specifically those who are most vulnerable. As we will see, these particulars provide means for critiquing society's judgments about care provision, humanity, and the good from a theological perspective. On this account, it is clear that Christian spirituality has shaped and continues to shape Vanier's life, writings, and the emergence of L'Arche.

L'Arche: A Sketch

Following the signs of the Spirit in early August 1964 Vanier responded to the needs of his time and invited three men with disabilities to live with him in a small house in Trosly, France.[58] The

56. Whitney-Brown, *Jean Vanier*, 27–29.

57. Vanier, *Our Journey Home*, viii. See Vanier, *Becoming Human*, 6; Vanier, *From Brokenness to Community*, 11.

58. Whitney-Brown, *Jean Vanier*, 30. In chapter 3 on "Mission" within *Community and Growth*, Vanier locates both his and L'Arche's responsiveness

community was named L'Arche, the Ark, after Noah's ark. Vanier writes, "The community of L'Arche wants to provide a refuge for people with mental handicaps, who can so quickly be drowned in the waters of our competitive society."[59] From its inception Vanier sought to organize L'Arche with restorative social forms that empowered persons with disabilities to cultivate and joyfully reclaim their full humanity. Reflecting on the aims of L'Arche, Vanier writes, "We seek to restore to people with handicaps their own particular humanity, the humanity which has effectively been stolen from them."[60] L'Arche exists not as a means of escape from society but rather as a place in which necessary time and opportunity are given to enable persons with disabilities find their place in society.

Since its genesis L'Arche has rapidly grown into a federation of 147 communities ranging across the globe in more than 35 countries on 5 continents.[61] Each community, though diverse in many ways, remains united around the commonly held vision that the humanizing gift of persons with disabilities to society becomes apparent in mutual relationships; a vision visibly expressed in drawing near, welcoming, and listening to others who are different from us.[62] Correspondingly, each community is grounded on welcome of the poor and on religious faith.[63]

For the duration of L'Arche a daily routine involving work, times for sharing meals, and celebration has been vital to both its structure and relationships. Commenting on the simplicity of the daily rhythm in L'Arche, Vanier writes, "[From the outset] we had our work in the house and garden (and later on in the workshops),

---

to this call in a grammar of having been called into the mission of the church. See Vanier, *Community and Growth*, 84–103; Reinders, "Being with the Disabled," 470.

59. Vanier, *Our Journey Home*, ix.

60. Ibid., xiii.

61. L'Arche International, "Our History."

62. Vanier, *From Brokenness to Community*, 38.

63. Ibid., 7. It is vital to note that the recurrent characterization of persons with disabilities as "poor" within Vanier's writings signifies "poverty of being" bestowed on them by cultural assumptions, judgments, and practices that are exclusionary, dehumanizing, and objectifying in nature.

and our meals together were often full of joy. We shared times of fun and relaxation and also prayer. As far as I was concerned, Raphaël and Philippe were not so much men with mental handicaps as friends."[64] Here, Vanier calls attention to how daily rhythm in L'Arche provides structure and a sense of belonging. Though simple in its form, the daily structure of L'Arche allows for the nurturing of genuine community that involves mutual support, togetherness, and friendship.

L'Arche stands in opposition to contemporary society in which privilege, power, and strength are held in high regard and perceived as indispensible attributes that constitute what it means to be human. L'Arche radically expresses a renewed vision for humanity in which difference is welcomed, otherness is valued, mutual support and trust define relationships, genuine community is possible, and weakness and vulnerability are given equal place at the table. Essentially, L'Arche offers individuals and society a new way of embodying a vision of peace that calls into question the undergirding powers and principalities currently effecting the characteristic spirit of this age.

In this chapter, we have focused on the characteristic spirit of the age in which L'Arche emerged, characterized L'Arche as the visible expression of Jean Vanier's faithful exploration of God's will in the course of his life, and outlined significant stages in Vanier's life that have been instrumental in the shaping of his spiritual and intellectual development, his writings, and the emergence of L'Arche and his work therein. In doing so we have focused on how Aristotelian thought has had an atmospheric impact on the development of Vanier's conceptual framework and the ways in which Aristotelian ethics underlie and shape Vanier's understanding of the meaning of what it means to be and become fully human in particular, together establishing certain intellectual trajectories and offering core beliefs that underlie his writings and work in L'Arche. Additionally, we have considered the place of Christian spirituality in the shaping of Vanier's life and writings and the emergence of L'Arche in order to better understand the role Christian faith and

64. Ibid.

the spiritual guidance of Père Thomas played in Vanier's intellectual and spiritual development, helping him discern the concrete
form God's call to take a path of peace in the course of his life
would take. These narratives of the inception, ethos, development, and organization of L'Arche, taken as a synthetic whole in
relation to Vanier's intellectual and spiritual development, not
only demonstrate the ways in which Vanier' thinking and L'Arche
epitomize a renewed vision of peace for humanity but also set the
stage for identifying central theological, ethical, and anthropological features that underlie and shape the characteristic spirit and
communal impulses belonging naturally to Vanier's understanding of community; all of which will be investigated in subsequent
chapters.

2

Welcoming Reality

THERE ARE MANY UNIQUE attributes that distinguish the characteristic spirit of any community. This chapter traces some of the theological, anthropological, and ethical impulses that have and continue to play a vital role in the shaping of the communal ethos of welcome found within L'Arche and Jean Vanier's writings. Also, this chapter examines the place and role the self and community play in welcoming the truth of reality as it is revealed and given within Vanier's thinking on community. At a deeper level this chapter provides a lens by which we can focus on how the phenomenon of welcome is not only a sign of community life and trust in God's providence but also a conduit of God's presence in the world. Attending to the ways Vanier names welcome as a way of life shaped by one's listening and responsiveness to the other will help us identify how welcome cultivates both life and growth within community, one's life, and one's life in relation to community. Correspondingly, this chapter constructively analyzes how Vanier's thinking on community in connection with L'Arche's inability to welcome everyone provides an access point for understanding the ways in which weaknesses, boundaries, and limitations are inherent to both community and human life.

Reality as it *is*: the Self, Community, and Welcome

The illusion of the self

CENTRAL TO VANIER'S THINKING on community is the idea that society is in denial of the truth of reality, especially when truth involves being confronted with the reality of human vulnerability, weakness, and pain. Commenting on the ways in which persons mask the truth of reality, Vanier writes, "I have discovered that I have many filters within my own self where I select and modify the reality I want to welcome . . . I select what pleases me, boosts my ego and gives me a sense of worth. I reject that which causes inner pain or disturbance or a feeling of helplessness."[1] Like Vanier, society as a whole seeks to structure its own moral existence from the perspective of self rather than accepting the truth of reality as it is given. That is, each person possesses his or her own way of filtering reality so as to preempt encountering the truth of reality as it *is*. Underlying the impulse to modify reality is society's perception that the self is the measure of all things. Consequently, reading truth and reality from the perspective of self only accentuates the illusion that self-striving toward autonomy, self-actualization, and self-preservation and *gravitas* are virtuous ways to accept reality as it *is*—the state of things as they actually exist, as opposed to an idealistic or notional idea of them.[2] Paradoxically, what appears to

1. Vanier, *Community and Growth*, 265.
2. *Oxford English Dictionary*, 2nd ed., s.v. "Reality."

be truth and reality are mere illusions. As we will see, Vanier syntactically situates "reality" within a discourse on welcoming and accepting that which is true according to the reality of one's self, as it is given and revealed. In doing so, Vanier contrasts reality as it *is* from illusion, fantasy, and modes of existence in which persons deny the reality concerning their self while simultaneously accepting false ideas and/or beliefs that have no basis in reality.

According to Vanier, society is in danger of living out its moral existence in denial of fundamental truths concerning what it means to be and become human. Vanier writes, "It is easy in our time to be swallowed up in the stagnant waters of our society which constantly encourage us to look out for ourselves."[3] The currents of our time, for Vanier, pressure individuals and society to acquire wealth, seek for material well being, and strive for the expansion of trade without consideration for the welfare of others.[4] Correspondingly, the system of commercial propaganda influences and persuades society that these currents are virtuous and will yield genuine liberty. Commenting on the paradoxical nature concerning how the societal propagandistic voice and undercurrents of social life only accentuate the deep insecurity in the hearts of individuals and society at large, Vanier writes, "A society which accepts or is prone to accept this deceit . . . is surely on the road to the most serious degeneration."[5] Moreover, the possibility for suffering greater anxiety and insecurity is heightened when society and individuals flee from reality as it *is* and live a life based on illusions and falsehood.

Vanier writes, "The danger for any community and for every person is to live in illusions. We all do that as we shut ourselves off from others."[6] Communities and individuals must accept reality as it is given and revealed; they must cultivate time, space, and opportunity to attend and respond to that which is true and in

---

3. Vanier, *Eruption to Hope,* 10.

4. Ibid.

5. Ibid.

6. Vanier, *Community and Growth,* 134.

accordance with reality as it *is*. Truth, for Vanier, is reality.[7] Here, Vanier is reliant on American psychiatrist Morgan Scott Peck's work *The Road Less Traveled* in which Peck writes:

> That which is false is unreal. The more clearly we see reality of the world, the better equipped we are to deal with the world. The less clearly we see the reality of the world—the more our minds are befuddled by falsehood, misperceptions and illusion—the less able we will be to determine correct courses of action and make wise decisions ... [8]

Vanier utilizes Peck's account of "truth is reality" to develop his thinking on what it means to be and become human, to grow in our true humanity as persons. Vanier writes, "There is no growth when we live in falsehood and illusion; when we are frightened to let the truth be uncovered and seen by ourselves and by others."[9] Clearly, Vanier believes that our lives must be oriented by and to the truth of reality as it *is*. When our lives are properly oriented to the truth of reality there is a willingness to open our hearts to others, uncover our masks, and expose our fears, anxieties, prejudices, misperceptions, and vulnerabilities. Vanier writes, "We must open ourselves up to the truth and let it be revealed."[10] Only then can the self be released from the dominion of the powers and principalities undergirding the characteristic ethos of the present age, from those undercurrents of society that stimulate the drives toward autonomy and self-preservation, and from the propagandistic voice that praises the self-precarious way of life in illusion.

Opening ourselves up to the truth of reality as it is given and revealed is the concretization of welcoming God's providence that is so vital for our lives. According to Vanier, this is a process of liberation that opens us up and leads us to the discovery of our common humanity.[11] He writes:

7. Ibid., 135.
8. Peck, *The Road Less Traveled*, 44.
9. Ibid.
10. Ibid.
11. Vanier, *Becoming Human*, 5.

> [This discovery] is a journey from loneliness to a love
> that transforms, a love that grows in and through belong-
> ing . . . The discovery of our common humanity liberates
> us from self-centered compulsions and inner hurts; it is a
> discovery that ultimately finds its fulfillment in forgive-
> ness and in loving those who are our enemies. It is the
> process of truly becoming human.[12]

What is being implied here is the notion that to evade reality as
it is given is to deny truth; attending to and welcoming truth and
reality as it *is* is to live as fully human.

Essentially, Vanier calls into question the natural psychologi-
cal/spiritual impulse that urges us to escape the truth of reality by
emphasizing how welcoming reality as it is given is the visible
expression of attentiveness and responsivity to God's providence,
and thus characteristic of what it means to be and become human.
Commenting on how being human involves remaining responsive
to reality as it *is*, Vanier writes:

> To be human means to remain connected to our human-
> ness and to reality. It means to abandon the loneliness
> of being closed up in illusions, dreams, and ideologies,
> frightened of reality, and to choose to move toward con-
> nectedness. To be human is to accept ourselves just as we
> are, with our own history, and to accept others as they are
> . . . [T]o be human is not to be crushed by reality, or to be
> angry about it or to try to hammer it into what we think
> it is or should be, but to commit ourselves as individuals,
> and as a species, to an evolution that will be for the good
> of all.[13]

Reality, for Vanier, is "the first principle of truth."[14] Denying reality is ultimately a failure to acknowledge what it means to be human—that is, to welcome our humanness for what it is—to accept
ourselves just as we are and others as they are. To be human involves the welcoming of reality that involves listening, valuing, and

12. Ibid.
13. Ibid., 15.
14. Ibid.

responsiveness to that which is true and in accordance with the authenticity of others and ourselves. This involves a way of life that is inclined to and shaped by listening and remaining responsive to the truth of reality given and revealed. Rather than living on the periphery of ourselves in which we put forth superficial effort to mask the reality of our lives and all its entailments, Vanier calls communities, each individual, and society as a whole to work toward cultivating and deepening an ethos of listening that promotes a way of life characterized by welcoming reality as it *is*.[15] Vanier writes, "[We must] constantly work to deepen our inwardness and our contact with the silent places at the heart of our being where God lives."[16] Vanier's understanding of truth of reality encompasses a spiritual/psychological phenomenon that requires listening to reality as it *is* in relation to the heart of one's essence. This notion further substantiates the foregoing assertion that welcoming the truth of reality as it *is*, for Vanier, not only is the visible expression of attentiveness and responsiveness to God's providence but also characteristic of what it means to be and become human.

Commenting on the ways in which we learn to read the signs of becoming more human, Vanier writes, "Each one of us needs to work at searching for truth, not be afraid of it. We need to strive to live in truth, because the truth sets us free, even if it means living in loneliness and anguish at certain moments . . . Perhaps this search for truth is a process of letting ourselves be enfolded in truth."[17] This pursuit of truth, for Vanier, presupposes that genuine liberty is experienced when individuals, communities, and society welcomes the truth of reality as it is revealed and given. "It is only as we begin to integrate such a sense of reality more fully into our being" that individuals, communities, and entire societies can discover what it means to be and become human as well as have "new intimations of what *is*."[18] Hence, Vanier views "welcome of reality" as a life-giving phenomenon in which individuals, communities,

---

15. Vanier, *Community and Growth*, 139.

16. Ibid.

17. Vanier, *Becoming Human*, 15.

18. Ibid., 16.

and society at large become more fully human as they commit to the truth of reality as it *is*. In view of the overall framework of Vanier's writings, "reality as it *is*" involves others; and thus, genuine liberty is about welcoming and being claimed by others. Therefore, one's abstract liberty is expressed as concrete attentiveness, responsiveness, and submission to another.

Underlying Vanier's thinking on the linkage between welcoming reality as it *is* and becoming human is the theological conviction that God is the primary object of humanity's moral existence and search for truth. Vanier characterizes reality as it *is* with a theological grammar in which truth engenders personal awareness of intrinsic poverty and sinfulness.[19] "Sinfulness" is a theological term internal to the logic of Christian faith. Contextually, Vanier integrates sinfulness with intrinsic poverty as a way to emphasize the poverty of being that is characteristic of human nature. In showing the relationship between the self-precarious life in which illusion, sinfulness, and poverty are inherent to humanity's being, Vanier accentuates how opening oneself up to the truth of reality as it *is* involves dependency on the Other, Jesus. Vanier writes, "[We] must cry out to Jesus, the Saviour, who will send us his Spirit and guide us, and forgive us. Only then can the truth make us free."[20] Ultimately, Vanier reads truth and reality from a christologically theocentric perspective that takes God as the primary object of moral inquiry. Truth and reality as it *is* is truth that God offers in Christ by means of his Spirit. Hence, welcoming truth and reality as it *is* holds the capacity to providentially lead one to an awareness of their inner poverty of being and sinfulness.[21] Additionally, "humanity," for Vanier, is read from the perspective of Christ. Crying out to Jesus is a visible expression of one's conscientiousness of their need to depend upon God. Cen-

19. Vanier, *Community and Growth*, 135.

20. Ibid.

21. By way of employing theological grammar Vanier provides thematic parallel constructions in which "illusions" and "falsehood" are contrasted with "providence," "truth," and "reality" and "closure" and "sinfulness" are opposed to "openness," "freedom," and "forgiveness" and the societal ethos of the current social life is contrasted with the "Spirit of Christ."

tral to this phenomenon is the belief that what it means to be and become human can only be read from the perspective of Christ. It is because Christ claims humanity that individuals, communities, and society at large can let itself be enfolded in truth, allowing Jesus to penetrate us, to give us new life.[22] Vanier writes:

> Jesus was sent by the Father not to judge us and even less to condemn us to remain in the prisons, limitations and dark places of our beings, but to forgive and free us, by planting seeds of the spirit in us . . . [T]rue growth comes from God, when we cry to him from the depths of the abyss to let his Spirit penetrate us . . . The stages through which we must pass in order to grow . . . are the stages through which we must pass to become more totally united to God.[23]

God, for Vanier, is the means by which persons and communities are able to fully live out their humanity in a way leading to growth and communion with God. Ultimately, to deny the truth of reality is to deny oneself of true welcome, growth, and communion with God. The illusion of self is a profound abandonment of our humanness, the humanness of others, and God's activity within the story of human existence.

The question of community

This section will emphasize the ways in which community, according to Vanier, is not an ideal place from which humanity is protected from falsehoods and illusions. When Vanier suggests the idea that community possesses the capacity to give life he does not mean that community is a solution to the weakness, vulnerability, and limitation characteristic to human nature. Nor is community a place that enables a person to avoid acknowledging and/ or encountering unpleasant, ominous, or threatening features of reality. Community is neither the means of eliminating nor the

---

22. Vanier, *Becoming Human*, 15; Vanier, *Community and Growth*, 133.

23. Vanier, *Becoming Human*, 15.

cure-all for an illusory and self-centered way of living. Instead community accentuates these realities. Although community can be life-giving, "it is also a place of pain because it is a place of truth and of growth."[24] Because community is the place of communion and relatedness to others and God, it is a place in which persons encounter reality as it *is*, given constraints. Vanier writes, "This permits them to start lifting their masks and barriers and to become vulnerable . . . But then too, as they lift their masks and become vulnerable, they discover that community can be a terrible place, because it is a place of relationship; it is the revelation of our wounded emotions and of how painful it can be to live with others."[25] Entering into community allows persons to begin the process of welcoming reality as it *is*, given constraints; a process that involves discovering and accepting that "the greatness of humanity lies in the acceptance of our insignificance, our human condition and our earth."[26] What is being implied here is that the discovery and welcome of the reality of one's own vulnerability are integral to making genuine community possible. True community and growth, for Vanier, can only occur when individuals within community and each community as a collective whole discover and welcome reality as it *is*, given constraints. Moreover, "true community implies a way of life, a way of living and seeing reality."[27] It involves a lifelong process requiring commitment to a way of life predicated on the discovery and welcome of reality as it *is*.

The process of welcoming reality as it is given and revealed is not an easy state of affairs. It involves encountering the revelation of our vulnerabilities, fears, and deep satisfactions derived from the perception we possess of ourselves. Community, for Vanier, "is the place where our limitations, our fears, and our egoism are revealed to us. We discover our poverty and weaknesses, our inability to get on with some people, our mental and emotional

24. Vanier, *From Brokenness to Community*, 10–11.

25. Vanier, *Community and Growth*, 25–26.

26. Ibid., 109.

27. Ibid.

blocks, our affective or sexual disturbances, our seemingly insatiable desires, our frustrations and jealousies, our hatred and our wish to destroy."[28] Community is the place that makes known reality as it *is*. On this account, community is not a place of unspoiled paradise in which persons live in a utopian state of relatedness. Rather, it is the place in which arise our impulses to self project and dominate, to mask our weakness, to consume others, and "do" things for others. Vanier writes, "While we are alone, we could believe we loved everyone. Now that we are with others, living with them all the time, we realize how incapable we are of loving, how much we deny to others, how closed in on ourselves we are."[29] Ultimately, community is the place of encounter in which encountering the other facilitates time, space, and opportunity leading to the discovery of our deepest self-centeredness, anguish, and poverty of being—the discovery of truth(s) concerning our "false" self.

Often accompanying the experience of encountering one's deep anguish and poverty of being are psychological and emotional conditions in which persons perceive themselves as lacking any ability to love and/or be present-*for* others. Vanier writes, "If we are incapable of loving what is left? There is nothing but despair, anguish, and the need to destroy. Love then appears to be an illusion. We are condemned to inner isolation and death."[30] This realization can give rise to feelings of despondency and defeatism leading to the loss and/or absence of hope. One way of responding to this inner pain and profound anguish, for Vanier, is to deny reality as it *is*. Vanier writes, "And from this anguish can be born many things . . . For when I am in this state of anguish I try to escape it by refusing life and reality."[31] This phenomenon is characteristic of what Vanier calls "falling into serious psychosis" in which one cuts their self off from the truth of reality as it *is* and enters into a world of illusions.[32] The self attempts to find a way of escape from inner

28. Ibid., 26.
29. Ibid.
30. Ibid.
31. Vanier, *Eruption to Hope*, 26.
32. Ibid.

isolation and death, conscious conflict, and anxiety. In a delusory manner, the self superficially copes with reality by way of denying the actual truth of reality. Consequently, this phenomenon only further exacerbates the set of conditions that initially led to the self's enclosure of itself in upon itself.

Rather than opening oneself up to the truth of reality as it *is,* the self is tempted to conceal the revelation of its poverty of being and declares its loyalty to a world of illusions and fantasy. In a way paralleling Havel's reflections on life in totalitarian states in which the individual supports their own victimization of living within the lie of life, Vanier portrays a reality in which the individual is capable of denying reality as it *is* thus enveloping one's self in an illusory life in which "living within the truth" becomes an existential, noetic, moral, and political threat to self-conscious creaturely existence.[33] This phenomenon is analogous to Friedrich Nietzsche's description of the lie: "I call a lie: wanting *not* to see something one does see, wanting not to see something *as* one sees it . . . The most common lie is the lie one tells to oneself; lying to others is relatively the exception."[34]

In order to further substantiate how this phenomenon is found to be present within community, Vanier places emphasis on what he sees as inevitable crises we encounter within the life of community. Commenting on the second crisis, which "is the discovery that the community is not as perfect as we had thought, that it has its weaknesses and flaws," Vanier writes, "The ideal and our illusions crumble; we are faced with reality . . . And the fourth is the hardest: our disappointment with ourselves because of all the anger, jealousies, and frustrations that boil up in us."[35] Since community is the place that makes known reality as it *is,* community does not necessarily impart life in the absence of vulnerabilities

33. Havel, "The Power of the Powerless." Here, I have chosen to employ Havel's suggestion that the individual is both victim and advocate of living within the lie and how illusions are spread throughout all dimensions of reality—existential, noetic, moral, and political to name a few.

34. Nietzsche, *The Twilight of the Idols and The Anti-Christ,* 185.

35. Vanier, *Community and Growth,* 136.

and constraints. Community possesses the capacity to threaten the illusory life in which dreams, appearances, and hallucinations mask reality as it *is*. For these reasons, community is not necessarily a way of escape from living an illusory life.

In view of the foregoing account concerning how community is a place that not only makes known reality as it *is* given constraints but also is a place of pain, I will briefly highlight Vanier's emphasis on the significance of the attempt to understand our own vulnerability as a key to genuine community; an emphasis that emerged from what Vanier identifies and describes as the "second call." Vanier writes, "The second call comes later, when we accept that we cannot do heroic things . . . [I]t is a time of renunciation, humiliation and humility. We feel useless; we are no longer appreciated . . . [T]he second call is often made at night. We feel alone and are afraid because we are in a world of confusion . . . We seem deeply broken in some way."[36] The second call, for Vanier, originated in his encounter(s) with persons experiencing severe disabilities and, in particular Lucien who "was paralyzed, incontinent, could not walk or speak, was cared for by his mother. His father had died when he was young. One day his mother was sent to the hospital. Thinking he was abandoned, Lucien howled in anguish. And Lucien came to live with us."[37] "Sometimes he [Lucien] used to howl as if he would never stop. His cries were very high-pitched; they pierced me like a sword. I could not bear them. I would have liked to have killed Lucien, to have hurled him out of the window," reports Vanier.[38] He continues, "I would have liked to have run away but I could not because I had responsibilities in the house. I was filled with shame and guilt and confusion."[39] Although some persons "invited him to interior silence" and "called forth love," Lucien led Vanier to the discovery of his own limits, inner anguish, and extreme vulnerability.[40] Commenting on the

36. Ibid., 139–40

37. Vanier, *Our Journey Home*, 75–78.

38. Spink, *The Miracle, the Message, the Story*, 176–80.

39. Ibid.

40. Ibid., 177–78.

darker moments of encountering the vulnerability of others and, in particular, Lucien's poverty of being, Vanier writes:

> I too became anguished. His closing up on himself would make me do the same. His violence and aggression aroused my own. And I was horrified to discover the sources of violence within my own self, to discover that in certain circumstances I myself could do harm to a weaker person. At certain moments, I touched the sources of psychological hatred within me. I could understand how a human being could try to hurt and destroy another. I saw how the weak person can draw out what is beautiful in me but also what is worst.[41]

Correspondingly, Vanier continues:

> For me, Lucien was an enemy. His cries of anguish revealed my own anguish; anguish which seemed to fill my body and make by heart pound until it was difficult to breathe. I never hit poor, weak Lucien, because I was not alone. I was in a milieu which protected me, a milieu which required me to observe certain rules, otherwise I would have been disgraced, judged, made to feel ashamed of myself. I am not saying that, if I had been alone, I would have hit Lucien, but it is clear that the community with all its rules and my need of respect helped me to contain my violence. But this painful experience with Lucien helped me feel solidarity with a lot of men and women in prison. When their inner violence was aroused by another person, they were not protected by a milieu which supported humane rules. So their violence led them to hurt or to kill. They were then condemned and humiliated. I was protected. But fundamentally there is no difference between us.[42]

Rather than always offering an ideal place of comfort and joy devoid of any anguish and pain, life in community and, in particular, living in community with Lucien not only engendered encountering the extreme otherness of the other [Lucien] but also Vanier's

41. Ibid., 179.
42. Vanier, *Our Journey Home*, 75–78.

discovery of his deepest anguish and poverty of being—a discovery of truth(s) concerning his true self. Emerging from his experiences in La Forestière Vanier would begin to further emphasize the significance of the attempt to understand our own vulnerability as a key to genuine community. As we will later see, vulnerability possesses a central place and role within Vanier's thinking on community as well as in L'Arche.

Although community can engender the discovery of one's profound limits it can also lead to true human growth and inner freedom. Of course community does not decisively control one's responsiveness to reality as it *is*; however, it can serve as a catalyst for genuine growth and inner freedom. Commenting on the "deep significance of community," Vanier describes community as a place that provides persons the opportunity to join in with the life of others "where they can develop their human and spiritual potential as fully as possible in a spirit of freedom and openness."[43] This notion presupposes that each individual constituting the community as a whole is also involved in the process of being and becoming more human. Thus, community provides a place in which opportunity is given to accept reality as it *is,* allowing the masks to fall and egoism to die. Vanier writes, "Community is the place where the power of the ego is revealed and where it is called to die so that people become one body and give much life . . . As all the inner plains surface, we can discover too that community is a safe place."[44] Therefore, community is essential for human growth. It is the place where persons can become truly human because it is the place in which the truth of reality as it *is*—who we really are—is revealed. Community is the place where each individual can become who they really are.[45] "Communities provide the 'soil' in which we can put down our roots," writes Vanier. "Without good 'soil', we cannot live and grow as human beings."[46] This presupposes that transformation does not flow from flight from reality but from

43. Ibid., 176.

44. Vanier, *Community and Growth,* 27.

45. Vanier, *Our Journey Home,* 178.

46. Ibid.

appropriating reality as it *is* and letting it transform the truth of who we are.[47] Commenting on human growth that originates from encountering the truth of reality of who we are, Vanier writes, "It is then, as we grow gradually into the acceptance of our wounds and fragility, that we grow into wholeness, life begins to flow forth to others around us."[48] Human growth then stems from the losing of illusions and by way of gradual death of the false self.[49] Accepting reality as it *is* leads to gradual transformation, growth, and freedom. On the whole community and the reality it can reveal to oneself and others can either crush the spirit of being and becoming human or play an *anastatic* role in which opportunity, time, and space is given to welcoming, or more precisely, listening and remaining responsive to reality as it *is*.

With its capacity to reveal the truth of reality as it *is* community can become a place of liberation and transformation. True growth, for Vanier, has its origin in God. Underlying Vanier's thinking on the relationship between community, human growth, and genuine transformation is the theological belief that becoming fully human presupposes welcome emanating from welcoming the Spirit of Christ to grow in us. Commenting on the source of growth in individuals and community, Vanier writes, "We can only emerge . . . if the Spirit of God touches us, breaks down barriers and puts us on the road to healing . . . To grow . . . is to allow this Spirit of Jesus to grow in us."[50] On this account, the growth and transformation originating from appropriating the truth of reality as it *is* takes on a spiritual dimension "when we allow Jesus to penetrate us, to give us new life . . . True growth comes from God," writes Vanier.[51] Commenting on the hope of this form of growth Vanier continues, "The hope is not in our own efforts to love. It is not in psychoanalysis which tries to throw light on the knots and

47. Vanier, "L'Arche—A Place of Communion and Pain," 16–17.

48. Vanier, *Be Still and Listen*, 61.

49. Vanier, *Community and Growth*, 136. See Vanier, *Becoming Human*, 120–22.

50. Vanier, *Community and Growth*, 131–33.

51. Ibid., 133.

blocks of our life, nor in the structures which have their effects on our personal lives. All this is perhaps necessary. But true growth comes from God . . . Growth in love is growth in the Spirit."[52] By way of placing growth in relation to both love and the work of the Spirit Vanier clarifies the ways in which growth is not an abstraction and/or an end unto itself. Appropriating reality as it is revealed and given is not the goal that is pursued in its own right to the exclusion of others. Rather, it allows time, space, and opportunity for growth that is embedded (pulled out of itself) in relation to love *for* others. In other words, the power of the ego is revealed and disarmed for the purpose of others. According to Vanier this whole operation is made possible via the active work of God in the story of human existence.

Vanier locates his speech concerning growth in love within community using a grammar that relates to a series of actions in which persons move from one particular condition at a specific time to another. Vanier writes, "The stages through which we must pass in order to grow in love are the stages through which we must pass to become more totally united to God."[53] This movement is from a state of oblivion into an encounter with reality as it *is*, given restraints. Encountering reality as it is revealed and given provides opportunity for the self to discover its desire to dominate, possess, and compete with others. Rather than failing to resist the same spirit that influenced Sartre's ill-judged embrace of the false self and fatalistic realism in which persons are held captive to a reality of power struggle, possessive love, and competition,[54] Vanier subverts Sartre's basic ontology concerning power struggle, emphasizes the in-breaking of Christ's claim on humanity, and says "no" to allowing one's reality to be defined by love that "masks the need to be superior to others" and "is only one person's freedom eating up another's freedom."[55] For Vanier, Sartre reads love from

52. Ibid.

53. Ibid.

54. Vanier, *Becoming Human*, 36. See Vanier, *Community and Growth*, 270.

55. Vanier, *Becoming Human*, 36.

the perspective of conflict in which persons struggle to project love upon the other until one person acquires as a result of a contest the other's dependency. As a result, lateral relationships are undergirded and influenced by possessive love, competition, and power struggle in which persons seek to work themselves over on everyone else. Humanity, for Vanier, neither exists for the purpose of living and dying in conflict, nor does the quality of being benevolent merely mask "the need to be superior to others."[56] Contrary to Sartre, Vanier emphasizes the false self's need to be displaced by the work of the Spirit. On this account, reality as it *is* is either a point for steeling oneself to become more powerful or repentance and submission to someone outside of oneself to be led into other people. Vanier points to God's activity in the story of human existence in relation to community and growth that leads to another state in which persons are given opportunity, time, and space to move from the state of discovering the truth of oneself to listening and remaining responsive to the reality of God's activity within the story of human existence. This movement presupposes that lateral non-competing reciprocity between persons is sustained by means of attentiveness and responsiveness to the Spirit of God. More so, the in-breaking of Christ's claim on humanity and the work of the Spirit of God displaces the false self and makes possible a community comprising open relationships that are not possessive, relationships that give life to others rather than ones turned in upon themselves, which undermine others in their search for wholeness.[57] Consequently, Vanier calls the conditions and spirit that influenced Sartre to dramatize Garcin's famous utterance: "Hell is—other people" into question and offers a vision of community and growth in which God's ways with mankind in the story of human existence offer new ways of being and belonging to others which makes community possible.[58] At a deeper level, dependency not autonomy; for Vanier, is what is means to be and become fully human.

56. Ibid.

57. Vanier, *Community and Growth*, 270.

58. Sartre, *No Exit*, 45. See Vanier, *Eruption to Hope*, 27.

Welcome as Sign of Community Life

Welcome plays a prominent role in Vanier's understanding of community. Welcome is vital for a community. Welcome is a sign of human growth and inner contentment with reality as it *is*, a visible expression of love and sign of peace.[59] Theologically speaking, welcome "is one of the signs of true human and Christian maturity," the concretization of trust in God's providence, and a conduit of God's presence.[60] Welcome engenders an encounter in which listening, understanding, trust, mutuality, and valuing otherness occur. Welcome is the beginning of growth. If welcome is absent in community, there is no growth.[61] Vanier's belief presupposes that welcome is not so much a singular act as it is a way of life that is inclined to listening and remaining responsive to otherness. Welcome cultivates life and growth within community; it is a sign that a community is alive.[62]

Community is by definition a place of welcome. However, if the individuals within community have not welcomed the community as it is and the members as they are then the welcome of others will not be genuine.[63] An unwillingness to live out one's fidelity to the concrete claim that others within the community lay claim to one's being affects his or her ability to genuinely welcome others outside the community. This applies to both individuals and community as a whole. Therefore, true welcome involves more than the visible expressions of invitation and reception of others. Genuine welcome entails an interiority of the heart. Vanier writes, "The welcome a community offers visitors is an extension of the welcome its members offer each other. If our heart is open to our brothers and sisters, it will also be open to others. But if we are

---

59. Vanier, *Community and Growth*, 265–73.

60. Ibid.

61. Vanier, discussion.

62. Vanier, *Community and Growth*, 266

63. Ibid., 272.

withdrawn from other members of the community, we are likely to close ourselves off from visitors."[64]

Welcome as an interiority of the heart is not achieved as a matter of course. It requires more than individual and collective acknowledgement, amenable treatment, and/or sociable response toward others. It involves more than welcoming the community as it is and others as they are. Certainly these phenomena are characteristic of welcome; however, welcome as an interiority of the heart is a phenomenon that involves a personal attentiveness to and acceptance of one's self. It requires one's willingness to open the door of their heart to the reality of who they are. Vanier writes, "To welcome is to be open to reality as it is, with the least possible filtering."[65] Accepting reality and one's place within it is not an easy task. In the same manner in which one gives the space for others to be and grow one must allow the necessary time and opportunity for themselves to grow to accept who they are and their place of being.

It is important to note that what is being implied here is not self-centeredness. Instead, personal attentiveness and acceptance of one's self, for Vanier, are means of breaking out of a self-centered way of life in which fears and illusions of reality "are as oppressive to others as they are to ourselves."[66] Accepting the reality of one's self and place of being is a necessary phenomenon that enables one to welcome community as it is and others as they are. Vanier writes, "To be human means to remain connected to our humanness and to reality. It means to abandon the loneliness of being closed up in illusions, dreams, and ideologies, frightened of reality . . . To be human is to accept ourselves as just as we are, within our own history, and to accept others as they are."[67] To deny ourselves as we are is to deny a part of our being.[68] Denial of self is a form of self-centeredness insofar as denial of self prevents genuine wel-

64. Ibid.

65. Ibid., 265

66. Vanier, *Becoming Human*, 15.

67. Ibid.

68. Ibid., 40.

come of the other. If welcome is to be open to reality as it *is*, then one must be willing to open the door of their heart to the reality of who they are.[69] It is when one begins to accept the reality of who one is and one's place of being within the story of human existence that genuine welcome of the community as it is and others as they are become possible.

For Vanier, accepting the reality of one's self and place of being does not occur in isolation. Instead, this phenomenon involves community in which one discovers one's self in relation to the other. "We do not discover who we are, we do not reach true humanness, in a solitary state; we discover it through mutual dependency, in weakness, in learning through belonging."[70] What is being implied though not explicitly expressed is that one's "self" is constituted by others. In the same way a healthy body is necessary for the healing of a wound, community is indispensable for one's discovery, acceptance, and welcome of the self.[71] Vanier writes, "Community life is the special place in which we come to know ourselves in truth."[72] Thus, there is a type of reciprocal phenomenon that occurs in community. Both the other and I participate with one another in welcoming each other while simultaneously receiving the welcome of the other. As we welcome and receive the others' welcome both the other and I begin to discover, accept, and welcome the otherness of ourselves. Here, I am naming what Vanier describes as "strangeness" and "brokenness" in addition to all the entailments linked to these realities as "the otherness of ourselves." Corresponding to my analysis above, Vanier states, "As we live with people in community and as we being to welcome the stranger, we will gradually discover the stranger inside us. When we welcome the broken outside, they call us to discover the broken inside."[73] On this account, discovering, accepting, and welcoming who I am and the reality of my place of being in the story of hu-

69. Vanier, *Community and Growth*, 265.

70. Vanier, *Becoming Human*, 41.

71. Vanier, *Man and Woman God Made Them*, 26.

72. Ibid., 78.

73. For more on these particulars see Vanier, "The Vision of Jesus," 67.

man existence requires relatedness to others. This contention is further substantiated by Vanier's claim, "At the heart of [community as] belonging is the fact that we have received our existence from others."[74] It is by means of attentiveness and acceptance to this reality that one begins to discover how to welcome one's self, community as it is, others as they are within community.

Risk always accompanies welcome. Vanier writes, "It is always a risk to welcome anyone and particularly the stranger. It is always disturbing."[75] The otherness of the other can be an unexpected and disturbing reality that interferes with the current arrangement and functioning of an individual or community. In welcoming the visitor, guest, friend, and stranger, a community and individual welcome the reality of who they are and their place of being in addition to all their ideologies and particularities, which can lead to disruption, intrusion, suffering, confrontation, and fear. Welcome presupposes an individual and/or community's willingness to be vulnerable.

The risk of welcome is both a promise of growth and life. More so, it is the visible expression of a community and/or individual's welcoming the providence of God, trusting God's ways within the story of our lives. Commenting on the risk of welcome, Vanier writes, "We have to remember that God is at the origin of everything."[76] A high theology of providence, for Vanier, provides the hope, confidence, and boldness needed to take risks to welcome and accept the otherness of the other as well as remain attentive to and endure any disturbances that result from the sphere of welcome and encounter. It is important to note that disturbances, in general, are not exclusive to the consequences of disagreements or confrontations emerging from encounters between persons. Although these realities are included in what is being conveyed, disturbances also relate to both the other and the otherness of the other themselves. Both the other and the otherness of others, by definition, possess the capacity to disturb another. Vanier writes,

74. Vanier, *Becoming Human*, 44.

75. Vanier, *Community and Growth*, 266.

76. Ibid., 162.

"One of the risks that God will always ask of a community is that it welcomes visitors, especially the poorest people, the ones who disturb us . . . The day the community starts to turn away visitors and the unexpected, the day it calls a halt, is the day it is in danger of shutting itself off from the action of God."[77] Hence, welcome involves listening and remaining responsive to God's activity in creation. It demands a great degree of attentiveness and availability to receive the reality of others as well as the inherent risks that accompany the otherness of the other. Vanier writes, "[Welcome] demands a quality of attentiveness, . . . an awareness of daily reality with all its unexpected happenings and insecurity."[78]

The limits of welcome

To suggest the idea that L'Arche has limitations to welcoming others may seem unsympathetic and/or overcritical. However, L'Arche's ability to welcome others is limited in scope. L'Arche has not, does not, and cannot welcome all persons into its community. In fact, one of the aims within the "Charter of the Communities of L'Arche" reads, "L'Arche knows that it cannot welcome everyone who has a mental handicap."[79] From the beginning, L'Arche has possessed and experienced limits to welcoming others. At its inception there were three men that accompanied Vanier. However, Dany, the third person who came to live with Vanier, Raphaël, and Philippe was unmanageable. Reflecting on Dany's disruptive behaviors that would immediately result in his expulsion from L'Arche, Vanier recalls:

> In a state of total insecurity, Dany began to hallucinate. He ran out into the quiet streets of Trosly-Breuil and made menacing gestures at the uncomprehending passers-by. The night of 5–6 August was a memorable one for Jean. Failing to find the electricity meter, although there was one in the house as he was to discover a few days

77. Ibid., 161–62.
78. Ibid., 162.
79. Vanier, *An Ark for the Poor*, 148.

later, he and his companions spent the first night in darkness and turmoil with Dany constantly on the move and Jean Vanier unable to get any rest in his bed up in his loft . . . Next morning the practical side of him recognised that it was impossible for Dany to stay . . . From that very first founding night Jean Vanier experienced the need to make choices, and suffering; his own suffering and sense of failure and the suffering of the men who had come to live with him.[80]

In the tenebrous light of L'Arche's first night, Vanier was led to the discovery of both his own and L'Arche's vulnerability—their incapacity to meet the needs of Dany.[81] Consequently, Dany was sent back to live at the institution from which he came. Vanier writes, "Having spent years in confinement living under rules and a strict routine, Dany was completely lost, beside himself, and aggressive. After a sleepless night, [I] was forced to admit that Dany would not be able to live in the structure [I] was providing . . . [L'Arche] began with great fragility."[82]

"This was the beginning of L'Arche: a vision, a desire, and audacious risk, an immediate wrenching failure and a new wisdom gained even that first night."[83] Clearly, Dany did not make it because his behaviors were perceived as unmanageable by Vanier. Naturally, our inclination is to focus on Dany's behavior as the primary reason for his exclusion. "Dany" did not make it because "he could not" adjust to the disciplined structures Vanier put in place. In other words, we are tempted to fix our attention on the ways in which Dany's aggression and inability to cope quickly led to the undesirable situations leading to his expulsion. However, restricting interest to Dany's behavior fails to take into account what Vanier's rejection of Dany represents. Was Dany's expulsion from

80. Spink, *The Miracle, the Message, the Story*, 61.

81. Whitney-Brown, *Jean Vanier*, 30.

82. This citation was taken from "A man becoming human," an archived subpage within Jean Vanier's website—https://web.archive.org/web/20120527085451/http://www.jean-vanier.org/l-arche-giving-life.en-gb.97.0.news.htm

83. Whitney-Brown, *Jean Vanier*, 30.

L'Arche a complete failure? Or, was his rejection a sign of the limits and inherent vulnerability of a community's ability to welcome?

In view of the romanticization of L'Arche that tends to accompany certain firsthand accounts, biographies, and narratives concerning its history, the discussion of expulsion, isolation, and the boundaries of L'Arche remain conspicuously absent. In fact, the first expulsion of an original member within L'Arche has been written out of many of the practical and theological narratives concerning the beginnings of L'Arche. On this point it is vital to note that Vanier, as early as August 22, 1964, eighteen days after the inception of L'Arche, wrote in a letter: "On the fourth of August (the feast day of Our Lady of the Snows) our first *two* boys arrived, driven by Madame Martin, from an institution."[84] Correspondingly, Vanier will later reflect:

> When I came to Trosly-Breuil, that small village north of Paris, I welcomed Raphaël, and Philippe. I invited them to come and live with me because of Jesus and his Gospel. That is how L'Arche was founded. When I welcomed those *two* men from an asylum, I knew it was for life; it would have been impossible to create bonds with them and send them back to a hospital, or anywhere else . . . The cry of Raphaël and Philippe was for love, for respect, and for friendship; it was for true communion.[85]

While some may read Dany's exclusion as a failure on the part of Vanier, it is my contention that this rare account demonstrates that exclusion is sometimes necessary in light of the limits of a community's ability to welcome all persons who arrive. More so, these limitations extend beyond the internal boundaries related to the initial stages of community building prior to welcoming others as well as the danger of dispersal when communities feel they need to welcome everyone.[86] Every community possesses limitations

84. See Vanier, *Our Life Together*, 11. Italics mine.

85. Vanier, *Community and Growth*, 97. Italics mine.

86. Ibid., 265–67. Vanier writes, "There is a time for everything—a time to build community and a time to open its doors to others." This presupposes that communities will always need times of closure.

that prevent them from welcoming all persons they encounter. Vanier writes, "Each community has its own weakness, its limitations which are also its wealth. It is important to recognize these limitations; we have to know what our norms of welcome are, who can be accepted within them and who the community can truly help."[87] A community must be attentive to the community as it is, the individuals making up community as they are, and the person(s) who have come to visit and/or seek membership within the community.

Correspondingly, Vanier writes, "In order to welcome the other there must be a peaceful space in the hearts of those welcoming (individuals as they are) and a peaceful place (community as it is) of rest and growth . . . At the same time, the people welcomed must try to accept the community as it is, with the space offered."[88] This account presupposes that a community's inability to welcome involves several dimensions. Among these are a community's internal powerlessness to welcome one another and the community as it is. Additionally, the very distinct features characteristic of a community's being, that is, its ethos, traditions, structures, norms, and rules may prevent the welcome of others. Paradoxically, that which constitutes the distinct nature of the community—its wealth and strengths—can also turn out to be its own weakness. The opposite can also occur in which the community's limitations and weakness become its wealth.[89]

In addition to the foregoing limitations related to a community's inability to welcome, Vanier addresses how the lack of reciprocity and immoderate behaviors on the part of the newcomer can also prevent true welcome. Vanier writes, "If a newcomer only wants to change the community and get everything they can out of it, without any modification on their part, there can be no true welcome . . . We have no right to accept someone who refuses to accept others or community life with all that it implies."[90] Even

87. Vanier, *Community and Growth*, 269.
88. Ibid., 268.
89. Ibid., 269.
90. Ibid., 268–69.

though Vanier admits there are times in which the newcomer may play a major role in preventing true welcome from occurring he is careful not to place fault solely on the newcomer. Rather than placing exclusive attention on the newcomer's unhealthy expectations, lack of inner stability, and immoderate behavioral patterns, Vanier asks, "Can we in the community give that person the peaceful space and the elements they need to be at ease and to grow? And then will they, so far as we can know them after dialogue and prayer, really benefit from the community as it is?"[91] Here, Vanier shifts the focus from the newcomer back upon the community. His questions presuppose that the community always possesses some measure of responsibility when there can be no true welcome of the other. This notion is expressed in a letter to friends, family members, and supporters of L'Arche in 1968 in which Vanier writes, "There is also some sad news. We had to send Gerard, Jean-Pierre and Marceau back to the psychiatric hospital at Clermont. This is very painful and we ask you to pray for them. We hope that some day we will be able to welcome them back with us or else find another place for them where they will be happier."[92] At the time Vanier recounts, "They were quite violent and needed more contained surroundings."[93] Although these men could not find their place in the community, Vanier assigns responsibility for their exclusion to L'Arche. He explains, "When we saw we couldn't help them, we had to take them back to the psychiatric hospital."[94] On this account, it is clear that a community's inability to welcome others is multifaceted; exclusion is not always the result of the internal powerlessness of a community's incapacity to welcome one another nor does it stem from the distinct features and essential qualities of the community itself.

Instead, a community's inability to welcome can originate from a lack of discernment, leadership, and awareness of its own limitations/weaknesses or mission. Vanier exhorts communities

91. Ibid.

92. Vanier, *Our Life Together*, 46.

93. Ibid.

94. Ibid.

to practice "double discernment" when making decisions about receiving new members into the community. Discernment is a necessary part of the welcoming process. Vanier writes, "A community needs wise people to discern peacefully and prayerfully."[95] A community must practice discernment when deciding whether to welcome newcomers into the community. This involves careful attentiveness to the community as it is, the individuals within the community as they are, and the newcomer(s). Aware that a community cannot accept every newcomer, Vanier emphasizes the responsibility a community possesses to discern its structures, ethos, and mission as well as its limitations and weaknesses prior to addressing circumstances relating to the newcomer.[96] Vanier writes, "It is important [for a community] to recognize these limitations."[97] A community must critically reflect and carefully discern whether it is the best place for a newcomer's growth.

Careful thought about whether or not newcomers will experience true welcome and growth in a community involves time and sensitivity. Yes, there may be times in which a newcomer's presence might be incompatible with community life and part of the reason for their exclusion. Although a newcomer's presence may give rise to extreme difficulties, Vanier acknowledges and places ultimate responsibility for exclusion on limitations inherent in community. Vanier writes, "It is so much better to refuse someone at the outset because the community is conscious of its limitations, than to welcome him or her naively and then ask them to leave."[98]

Exclusion is sometimes necessary, though abandonment is never an option.[99] Saying no to a newcomer does not necessarily

---

95. Ibid.

96. Ibid., 268–69.

97. Ibid., 269.

98. Ibid., 275.

99. The notion of "necessary exclusion" as being integral to the discourse of "inclusion" is an emerging topic of interest within theology of disability discourse. Reinders and Swinton, "Frontiers in Theology and Disability"; Swinton, "Beyond Kindness," 20.

entail that the community relinquishes its responsibility for and/
or attentiveness to the one who is refused entry into the community. Instead, there are ways of saying no with care and concern
for the other. Vanier writes, "There is a way of taking time, listening, explaining why the persons cannot stay and offering sugges-
tions where he or she could go. It is such a wounding experience
to be turned away. We must always remember that."[100] It is my
contention that both the one excluded and the community experiences this wounding effect. Vanier writes, "There is something
prophetic in people who seem marginal and difficult; they force
the community to become alert, because what they are demand-
ing is authenticity."[101] But, when exclusion is necessary, it provides
a community opportunity, time, and space to reconsider its very
nature and authenticity to itself and others. That is, it forces a community to become attentive to its limitations and weaknesses.

Not only does this synthetic account of the practical and
intellectual development of Vanier's thinking on community life
provide a lens for us to see how weaknesses, boundaries, and limitations inherent to community life can prevent true welcome but
also how the same state of affairs that once forced Vanier to admit
both his own and L'Arche's fragility are now integrated within as
well as shape Vanier's thinking on community. It is my contention
that Dany's expulsion at the inception of L'Arche was not necessarily an all-out failure within the history of L'Arche but rather an
opportunity and sign of the limits and inherent vulnerability of a
community's ability to welcome. It was a prophetic moment in the
life of L'Arche that resulted in self and community conscientious of
its own limitations and fragility.

Assessment

To conclude our reflections, L'Arche's inability to welcome everyone
not only provides a new way of understanding how vulnerability is

---

100. Vanier, *Our Life Together*, 268.

101. Ibid., 274.

inherent to human life but also an essential characteristic of community life. Because community entails a way of life, community provides time, space, and opportunity for a new way of seeing the reality of one's self and others as they are. Community involves a great undertaking that calls for a lifelong commitment to faithful exploration, discovery, and welcome of reality as it *is*, given its constraints, thus making one's self and community possible.

In view of the foregoing analysis, community is a place where people can learn to discover and welcome their own vulnerability and brokenness. In the same way others must come to accept the reality of one's true self, Vanier had to come to discover and welcome the reality that L'Arche was, is, and will always continue to exist as a fragile reality. "L'Arche is a fragile reality," writes Vanier.[102] Vanier's discovery clues us in on the theological significance of encounter in which he was brought face to face with the unexpected experience of an unpredictable reality of realities of a long day that began with Dany's initial inclusion and spontaneous expulsion from L'Arche; a reality that would not only signify the fragile nature of what it means to faithfully explore God's will in remaining responsive to the cries of the poor but also how L'Arche paradigmatically reflects "the inescapable reality of insecurity" of life in all its variegations.[103] Hence, the theological significance of Vanier's encounter with reality is that fragility is an inescapable reality. To welcome reality as it *is*, given its constraints, is to welcome life as gift, accepting the fact of one's created self in relation to others; namely, God—the Other, and others.

On the whole, the fragility of L'Arche is its greatest strength.[104] The discovery and welcome of its own limits and vulnerability has proven to be the key to making L'Arche possible. Coming to terms with its own necessary fragility has enabled L'Arche—its individual members and the community as a whole—to listen and remain responsive to emerging limits throughout its past and present

102. See Vanier, "The Fragility of L'Arche and the Friendship of God," 25.

103. Whitney-Brown, *Jean Vanier*, 47.

104. Edmonds, *A Theological Diagnosis*, 194. Here, I am grateful for Edmonds's analysis on "the necessary incompleteness of L'Arche."

history.[105] As we will see in the following chapters, the necessary fragility of L'Arche has given definite shape to a radical vision and practice of care provision that presupposes that care possesses an intrinsic relationship to creaturely worship. Welcoming the inescapable reality of it's own fragility has enabled L'Arche to prophetically reveal to both church and world that how we care for others visibly expresses the measure of moral fiber concerning the church's understanding and act of worship.

105. Vanier, *An Ark for the Poor*, 72, 83, 92, 94. These pages portray both Vanier and L'Arche seeking to remain responsive to having to encounter their own limits, pain, and fragility.

3

Welcoming Otherness

OUR FOCUS IN THIS chapter is on vulnerability. Within L'Arche and Jean Vanier's writings, vulnerability encompasses persons with disabilities and handicaps, weakness and poverty, and otherness and strangeness. For this reason, the following chapter identifies and describes how vulnerability undergirds and informs Vanier's thinking on community as well as life in L'Arche. In what follows, an analysis of how the weak and poor in society are visible expressions of Christ's presence within the world will be given in order to draw attention to ways in which vulnerable persons are sources of life, unity, and communion with God and others.

On the Place of the Vulnerable
within Society and the Church

VULNERABILITY POSSESSES A CENTRAL place and role within
Vanier's thinking on community as well as life within L'Arche.
Emerging from both Vanier's writings and L'Arche is the recur-
ring message of the value of vulnerability as well as the prophetic
embodied witness of the significance of persons with disabilities
in society and in the church. In fact, the focal point of fidelity at
L'Arche "is to live with people who have a handicap, in the spirit
of the Gospel and the Beatitudes."[1] Undergirding this message is
Vanier's conviction that God calls each individual and community
to a general mission of responsiveness to God's activity in the story
of human existence. He writes, "There is the general mission for
each community and for each person to give life. However, each
community has its specific mission, its specific way of giving life
through its particular goals."[2] Contextually, Vanier locates mission
in relation to the ways in which certain communities within the
Christian tradition have responded to specific cries and needs
of humanity at particular moments in history.[3] Appealing to
Benedictine monasticism and its commitment to prayer, communities founded by Mother Teresa centered on the marginalized of
Calcutta, the Catholic Worker and Simon communities focused
on men and women who are down and out, and other individual

1. Vanier, *Community and Growth*, 150. See Spink, *The Miracle, the Message, the Story*, 265.

2. Vanier, *Community and Growth*, 88.

3. Ibid.

and communal expressions epitomizing what it means to remain responsive to the cries of humanity, Vanier writes:

> Each new community is called forth by God, as he inspires a particular man or woman or a group of people to respond to a specific cry or need of humanity at one particular moment of history . . . Each new community with its founder has a specific charism, gift and mission, responding to a particular cry for help, for recognition and for love.[4]

Vanier believes God has called both L'Arche and himself to listen and remain responsive to the particular cries for love, respect, friendship, and true communion arising from persons "who are weak and poor because of a mental handicap and who feel alone and abandoned."[5] He writes, "We enter community to live with others. But also, above all, we come to live the goals of the community with them, to respond to a call from God, to respond to the cry of the poor."[6] Central to this conviction is Vanier's understanding of God's covenant with the poor. Commenting on Exodus 2–3 in which God listened and responded to the cry of his people, Vanier writes, "And he [God] sent Moses to liberate them. Today as yesterday the covenant between God and the poor remains; he calls people to community to respond to the cry of the poor and the oppressed."[7] Vanier interprets God's liberating activity with Israel in a universal way as a means to identify the constant form of God's call and activity within the story of human existence. What is occurring in Israel's own time (Exodus 2–3), for Vanier, is occurring at all times. "In all ages and in many religions, people have come to life together, yearning and searching for God . . . Other communities—particularly those in the Christian heritage—were founded to serve the poor, the lost, the hungry and those in need."[8] Vanier reads the cries, anguish, and oppression of persons with

4. Ibid., 89.

5. Ibid., 97.

6. Ibid., 92.

7. Ibid., 92–93.

8. Ibid.

disabilities as current forms of the cries of God's oppressed people in Exodus 2–3. Vanier interprets Scripture for his age, identifies God's continual faithfulness toward humanity, and the poor and most vulnerable in particular, and models ways in which communities and individuals can listen and remain responsive to God and others by bearing witness to the concretization of the gospel in current situations. Vanier believes that to listen and remain responsive to the cries of the weak, poor, and most vulnerable and marginalized in society, specifically persons with disabilities, is to listen and remain responsive to the call of God.[9]

Accordingly, communion with the vulnerable and poor is communion with God. Commenting on what he perceives as a great secret of the Gospels and heart of Christ, Vanier writes:

> Jesus calls his disciples not only to serve the poor but to discover in them his real presence, a meeting with the Father. Jesus tells us that he is hidden in the face of the poor, that he is in fact the poor. And so with the power of the Spirit, the smallest gesture of love towards the least significant person is a gesture of love towards him.[10]

Jesus' presence is in the poor and most vulnerable. Appealing to Mathew 25, Vanier writes, "Jesus is the starving, the thirsty, the prisoner, the stranger, the naked, the homeless, the sick, the dying, the oppressed, the humiliated. To live with the poor is to live with Jesus; to live with Jesus is to live with the poor."[11] Communion entails a shared life with the poor in which "people come together not just to liberate those in need, but also to be liberated by them; not just to heal their wounds, but to be healed by them; not just to evangelise them but to be evangelised by them," writes Vanier.[12] Those perceived as being the weakest in society are a source of life and communion; they are conduits of the presence of Jesus.[13] The

9. Ibid., 93.

10. Ibid.

11. Ibid., 95.

12. Ibid., 96.

13. Ibid. See Spink, *The Miracle, the Message, the Story*, 63.

poor, persons with disabilities can be a paradox; strength lies at the heart of weakness. Vanier writes, "We realize that our shared life with them in L'Arche is a treasure. A secret has been entrusted to us. People with disabilities are a sign, a presence of Jesus and a call to unity. The weak and the poor are for us a source of unity."[14] Rather than being perceived as a source of shame or punishment from God persons with disabilities are a path toward God.[15] What is being implied here is that persons with disabilities constitute a place in which the mysterious presence of God, and God's hidden strength and power in weakness are found.

Persons with disabilities are an embodied witness of love within society and the church, and thus present a prophetic challenge for love in the face of society and the church. In the light of reason and responsibility combined with the domineering societal and individual pursuits of autonomy in which freedom has come to be synonymous with independence, persons with disabilities are "certainly failures," writes Vanier.[16] Commenting on how persons with disabilities are not autonomous and cannot achieve this type of freedom, Vanier writes:

> [Persons with disabilities possess] a weakness of the "self," that is of the rational and willful self. This rational self is necessary in order that we may be active in society, capable of organizing our lives and those of others. But man is not just a social being who has to struggle further in his place in society and defend himself, he also loves and wants to be loved, to communicate and to share. To be active in society it is imperative to have a strong integrated self.[17]

Clearly, Vanier believes this integrated self is lacking within a world in which contemporary society "is continually becoming harder, where men are obliged to work furiously to acquire riches, where kindness is not respected and is drowned in a mounting tide

14. Vanier, *Community and Growth*, 96.
15. Vanier, "Prepared Remarks."
16. Vanier, *Eruption to Hope*, 41.
17. Ibid.

of efficiency."[18] Within this society there are many persons who are efficient and powerful, "who have all the qualities to organize, to act and command," Vanier writes. However, "their hearts are atrophied, they have no compassion. They are too self-reliant and independent. They tend to regard other people as objects, or at best as inferior and without value . . . They are domineering and their consciousness of self is one of superiority."[19] Consequently, these persons lack the necessary responsiveness that allows them to listen and communicate with and have compassion for others.[20] Acting in accordance with the norms of society these persons, by means of reason and will, take their place in that society.[21]

It is vital to note here that Vanier does acknowledges the presence of others, despite their rational and willful self, who have maintained that sensibility that gives necessary time, space, and opportunity to listening and responsiveness to others. Vanier writes, "[These persons] are not afraid of human relationships. They have preserved that transparency and purity which make them attractive to others. Their open nature is appealing; a feeling of warmth and goodness emanates from them."[22] By way of contrasting qualities of rationality and will and the consciousness of power with alternative qualities that empower persons to welcome, listen, and remain responsive to others, Vanier emphasizes the limits of the rational self. Vanier writes, "The qualities which enable a man to accept another person and communicate with him, are not found in the rational self, but in a deeper self which corresponds to an aspiration to love which, however, can be suppressed and buried in the realm of the unconscious."[23]

Paradoxically, it is the lack of consciousness of power that empowers persons with disabilities to welcome, listen, and remain responsive, or more precisely, "love" others in a more perceptive

18. Ibid., 43.
19. Ibid., 41.
20. Ibid.
21. Ibid., 42.
22. Ibid.
23. Ibid.

and flourishing manner without delay. Commenting on how persons with disabilities can be a paradox, Vanier writes:

> They cannot be men of ambition and action in society and so develop a capacity for friendship rather than of efficiency. The are indeed weak and easily influenced, because they confidently give themselves to others; they are simple certainly, but often with a very attractive simplicity. Their first reaction is often one of welcome and not of rejection or criticism. Full of trust, they commit themselves deeply . . . Free from the bonds of conventional society, and of ambition, they are free, not with the ambitious freedom of reason, but with an interior freedom, that of friendship. Who has not been struck by the rightness of their judgments upon the goodness or evil of men, but their profound intuition on certain human truths, by the truths and simplicity of their nature which seeks not so much to appear to be, as to be. Living in a society where simplicity has been submerged by criticism and sometimes by hypocrisy, is it not comforting to find people who can be aware, who can marvel? Their open natures are made for communion and love.[24]

Vanier contrasts the inherent qualities of mind and character of persons with disabilities with the nondisabled persons' determination to achieve success that typically requires strong-mindedness, willpower, and hard work. In doing so, Vanier draws attention to the ways in which persons with disabilities are fit for *accomplishing* a distinct form of efficiency in a conventional society.[25] They have a special place within society; they play a vital role in the progress of the world. To say that persons with disabilities possess "a capacity for friendship rather than efficiency" is not to claim they are absolutely incompetent, or more precisely, unfit for a particular capacity. Instead, Vanier accentuates the distinctive attributes and

24. Ibid., 43.

25. "Efficiency" stems from the Latin word *efficientia*, which is based on the verb *efficere*, "accomplish." In order to draw attention to the way in which persons with disabilities are distinctly efficient from society's conventional understanding of what it means to be efficient I have emphasized the term "accomplishing."

characteristics possessed by persons with disabilities in order to call attention to the ways in which they make up what is lacking in that society. Therefore, persons with disabilities are "properly fit for" what Vanier calls, "restoring the balance of the virtues of sensibility and love," in a society shaped by powers and principalities that render it almost impossible to live out valuing others via friendship, welcome, commitment, and love.[26]

Though their lack of consciousness of power and rationality can often cultivate more profound anguish and internal suffering, persons with disabilities "are a sign, by their very being, that peace and joy, happiness in fact, are not gained by work alone, and do not depend on wealth," power of reason and will, or by way of societal norms influenced by efficiency, advancement, and/or competition.[27] Persons with disabilities are "capable of awakening what is most precious in a human being—the heart, generosity, the dynamism of love. They incite us to put our intelligence at the service of love. They have the capacity to heal others by calling them to unify within themselves their deep emotions, their capacity for love and their reason," writes Vanier.[28] Viewed in this light, persons with disabilities are a "constant reminder of the poverty and receptivity required by love, but also of wonderment, joy and peace which radiate from those who know how to receive and how to give," writes Vanier. Their profound vulnerabilities combined with their power to welcome, listen, remain responsive, and love call into question the powers and principalities undergirding the characteristic spirit of this current age, at the same time calling forth a true altruism from the false eminence of the autonomous self, both collective and individual, that holds power.[29] Persons with disabilities are not

26. Ibid., 44.

27. Ibid., 42–43. Vanier writes, "[Their] distress is much greater because they have no rational nature which could help them to overcome and adapt themselves more or less successfully in accordance with conventions and laws. And since no man can live in anguish, they become angry and violent, or sink into a state in which they refuse all contact with reality."

28. Vanier, *Man and Woman God Made Them*, 188.

29. Vanier, *Eruption to Hope*, 43.

failures at all but rather whole persons of great significance; they are sources of life.[30]

Appealing to the first epistle to the church at Corinth in which St. Paul writes, "God has chosen the weak and the foolish according to the world in order to confound the strong and so-called wise" (1 Cor 1:27), Vanier contends, "People with learning disabilities can be open to the message of Jesus which is essentially a message for the heart. That is why the message of Jesus gives ultimate meaning of [sic] the lives of people with disabilities."[31] What is being implied here is that the ways of God are not the ways of this world. Contextually, Vanier's believes the gospel reveals the ways in which God's ways with mankind overturn the "normate" perspectives concerning those whom society might consider weak and foolish.[32] Commenting on how the gospel "reveals the true meaning of the poor, the weak and the non-productive," Vanier writes, "The message of Jesus is clear: the Good News is announced to the poor. That good news is that they will never be abandoned; they are loved by the Father who takes care of them. They *do* have a place; they *do* have value."[33] The gospel reveals that human value does not depend upon strength and power or one's capacity to reason but rather on Christ's claim on humanity. Read from this perspective, persons with disabilities possess a quality of being that is worthy of great significance and value, which is not related to and/or dependent upon any utility they may offer to society and the church.

Contrasting what he perceives as the underlying impulses that give form to a society that marginalizes, oppresses, and discards those who are most vulnerable and seemingly non-productive

30. Vanier, *Man and Woman God Made Them*, 188.

31. Ibid., 3.

32. For more information on the "normate" within disability studies see Yong, *The Bible, Disability, and the Church*, 10–11. See Wynn, "The Normate Hermeneutical and Interpretations of Disability"; and Thompson, *Extraordinary Bodies*. Correspondingly, Hauerwas locates what many consider "normate" in a more critical register; namely, the "tyranny of normality," in "Community and Diversity."

33. Vanier, *Man and Woman God Made Them*, 189.

with certain spiritual dimensions of the gospel, Vanier writes, "The Good News is announced to the poor not to those who serve the poor."[34] Correspondingly, "The poor are at the heart of [a] new structure, the first place belongs to them, theirs is the Good News of the presence of Jesus, the Good News which is rejected," writes Vanier.[35] The charter of the gospel constitutes a political dimension that values all of creaturely existence, especially those whom society repudiates and gives last place, "if they [are given] a place at all."[36] The "politic" that shapes societies' gestures of giving the first places to the rich and powerful, to those who are productive and useful, socially stratifies weakness, poverty, and otherness to a place of no account, thus engendering inhumane gestures that frequently destroy persons with disabilities often at the moment of their birth if not before, cast them aside as they grow up, and result in the reluctance to provide them the last places therein. In contrast, the gospel presents a theological account of social organization in which those members with whom society refuses to accept and/or associate on the basis of utility function possess both a central place and role at the heart of its message.[37] By way of instituting a central place for the weak and poor at the heart of its message, the gospel invests the most vulnerable within society with a role of revealing the mystery of God's ways with mankind.

"The Gospel is crazy," writes Vanier. "It sees in the weak and the poor a sign and a sacrament of God, thus revealing the mystery of Jesus and leading us to a true inner freedom, through a community life with celebrations and relationships."[38] In a way analogous to Yves Congar's "sacrament of our neighbor," Vanier regards the weak and the poor as the concretization of divine presence in the world.[39] "The mystery of Jesus," for Vanier, is that Jesus is the weak

34. Vanier, *From Brokenness to Community*, 20.

35. Vanier, *Man and Woman God Made Them*, 123.

36. Ibid.

37. Ibid.

38. Ibid., 191.

39. Congar, *The Wide World My Parish*, 124. Congar writes, "But there is one thing that is privileged to be a paradoxical sign of God, in relation to

and poor.[40] "We are privileged, wherever we may be, no matter what our place in society, to be close to [persons with disabilities] around us . . . Being close to them, we are close to Jesus. That is the mystery, the secret of the gospel of Jesus: [They] render Jesus present," writes Vanier.[41]

Understanding the gospel this way opens up christological implications concerning the paradoxical signs of God in the world. Commenting on Jesus' identification with the least of these, "Whatever you did to one of the least of these my brethren, you did it to me" (Matt 25:40), Vanier writes, "Whoever visits a prisoner, clothes the naked, welcomes a stranger is visiting, clothing and welcoming God. This is a great mystery!"[42] Seeing the weak and the poor as visible expressions of Jesus' presence in the world, Vanier parts ways from the classical interpretation in which "the least of these" are exclusively translated as Christ's emissaries who encounter hardships in their missionary efforts.[43] Vanier reads this passage as a basic paradigmatic text in which "the least of these" universally applies to all the persons in the world who are poor, weak, marginalized, oppressed, and in need. In a way paralleling Gustavo Gutiérrez's "conversion to the neighbor," Vanier's reading of the gospel presupposes that Christ's presence concretized in the weak and poor "determines the visible shape of humanity's encounter(s) with God."[44] According to Vanier, the gospel declares that "the least of these" within society, far from being considered of no account, are central to society.[45]

---

which men are able to manifest their deepest commitment—our neighbor. The sacrament of our Neighbor!"

40. Vanier, *Community and Growth*, 95.

41. Vanier, *Befriending the Stranger*, 2.

42. Ibid., 4.

43. For a detailed account on what is commonly known as the classical interpretations of this passage see Luz, "Matthew: a Commentary," 263–96.

44. Gutiérrez, *A Theology of Liberation*, 194. Gutiérrez writes, "The modes of God's presence determine the forms of our encounter with him."

45. Vanier, Community and Growth, 308.

Another theological impulse shaping Vanier's thinking on the value, place, and role of the most vulnerable in society is St. Paul's description of the church as the community of the faithful, a living body made up of different parts. Appealing to 1 Corinthians 12:21–25, in which Paul speaks of the church as a body of different parts, Vanier writes, "Each one is important, not only because of their function and the fact that each one is unique and irreplaceable but also because when one member suffers, the whole body suffers . . . It is the same for the body of humanity: each member is different, each is important."[46] Extending the relevancy of Paul's exposition of Jesus' vision for the church to "the body of humanity," Vanier emphasizes the irreplaceable place of the most vulnerable within society as a whole. "Jesus came into the world to change and transform society from a 'pyramid' in which the strong and clever dominate at the top, into a 'body' where each member of society has a place, is respected, and is important," writes Vanier.[47] "Through this teaching," writes Vanier, "we see a vision unfold in which a pyramid of hierarchy is changed into a body, beginning at the bottom."[48] On this account, Paul's description of the church is more than a rhetorical figure of speech in which the church is conceptually regarded as symbolically representative of Christ's body. Instead, Vanier reads Paul's body imagery and call to wholeness in the body of Christ (1 Cor 12) in relation to Ephesians 4:15–16, taking into account what he sees as the all encompassing political "vision of Jesus for our world" in which Christ lays claim on all creaturely existence.[49] As a result of these interpretive moves, Vanier writes, "By his death and resurrection Jesus came to bring together this fragmented world of ours . . . Yes, this is the vision of Jesus for our world announced by St. Paul: one body—with the poorest and weakest among us at the heart, those that we judge the most despicable, honoured; where each person is important

46. Vanier, *Befriending the Stranger*, 38.

47. Ibid.

48. Vanier, "The Fragility of L'Arche and the Friendship of God," 31.

49. Vanier, *The Broken Body*, 67–68, esp. 74 in which Vanier describes Jesus' vision in terms of "a new vision for humanity, a new world order."

because all are necessary."[50] Consequently, Christ's body is an equalizing place to which all of humanity belongs.

When read from the perspective of Christ's creative and reconciliatory work, Paul's appeal to the Corinthian church to receive God's divine working within all the parts of its body, according to Vanier, paradigmatically reveals Christ's claim on "all" creaturely existence including the social body of humanity. At this point it is important to note that Vanier does not equate humanity with the church as the body of Christ. Instead, the pneumatological reality of which the body of Christ has been made part through God's creative and redemptive work, for Vanier, is how humanity is meant to be, and therefore stands as an invitation to all social reality in which all members of the "body of humanity" are placed. "Humanity," writes Vanier, "is called to know itself as one body."[51] On this account, Vanier tacitly assumes that all political bodies are broken; and thus, are called to wholeness, or more precisely, called to be "bodies" in which all its members have a place, are valued, and are important, given their constraints.[52] According to Vanier's reading of Paul's announcement of Christ's vision for the church, wholeness in the body of Christ—the church is made possible via the Spirit of God constantly giving specific form to its political existence. This is evidenced when each member welcomes God's divine working within "all" its parts. In the same way the effectiveness of Christ in his body is diversified by the functions of all its parts, the well being of "the body of humanity" is contingent upon the variegation of the place and roles of its individual members, especially those who are often relegated to no account.[53] Vanier sees the "body of humanity" moving toward wholeness when genuine welcome and value are extended to "all" its members, especially those we tend to hide; those members who, according to Vanier, are visible expressions of Jesus' presence. By way of rendering Jesus present *intus et extra ecclesiae*, the weak and the poor concretize

50. Ibid.
51. Vanier, *The Broken Body*, 100. See Brock, "Theologizing Inclusion."
52. Vanier, *Befriending the Stranger*, 38.
53. Orr and Walther, "1 Corinthians," 268.

the specific pneumatological form the Spirit of God gives to the body of Christ—the church, and the constant form of the presence of Christ manifest within the "body of humanity."[54]

Vanier's Theology of Community

In view of the foregoing account it is without contention that community is a central theme inherent in Vanier's writings. Community "is a wonderful place, it is life giving; but it is also a place of pain because it is a place of truth and of growth—the revelation of our pride, our fear, and our brokenness," writes Vanier.[55] Community is a place of togetherness, openness, caring, cooperation, healing and growth. It is a place where hope is held, forgiveness remains, trust is formed, peace is proclaimed, difference is welcomed and celebrated, and persons are enabled to become fully human.[56] On this account, community does not consist of spatial dimensions in which persons merely reside. Instead, community involves genuine presence and communion that emanates from real encounters between persons. It is a place of belonging that is "an integral part

54. Vanier, *The Broken Body*, 128–29. Vanier writes, "Since the day the Word became flesh and became one among us, each human being is intimately linked to Jesus. The Word became man in every way . . . Jesus is one of us, one of our flesh . . . Here lies the mystery. The body of Christ is humanity." At this point in his writing Vanier is emphasizing the "body," or more precisely, the mysterious presence of Christ concretized in those whom Christ identifies with in the Gospels (i.e., hungry, thirsty, imprisoned, sick, stranger, weak, and poor) rather than the "body of Christ"—the church. Even though his language is ambiguous, the context surrounding Vanier's phrasing evidences a clear distinction between the "body" of Christ (divine presence concretized in humanity) and the "body of Christ"—the church, the faithful "assembly of believers, those who have been called out of a world full of sin and hate and fear, but also to remain in it as a witness of love and a sign of the resurrection . . . Those who trust in Jesus, who recognize in him the Lamb of God who saves and heals, and frees us from guilt." For more theological account on Vanier's insistence on the relational coinherence of humanity and the life of God, see Hall, *An Inquiry into the Theology and Practice of Covenantal Living in L'Arche*, 60.

55. Vanier, *From Brokenness to Community*, 10–11.

56. Within this section I am taking into account the multifaceted communal themes running in the foreground of Vanier's works, on the whole.

of human nature. Isolated we shrivel up and die."[57] Community is essentially a way of life.

More specifically, community is "the place of meeting with God."[58] For Vanier, place is not a spatial category. Instead, place is described as the body of persons making up community in which encounters between persons are made possible via being, belonging, and living together. "I am talking essentially of groupings of people who have left their own milieu to live with others . . . and work from a new vision of human beings and their relationship with each other and with God," writes Vanier.[59] Commenting on Bonhoeffer's communal perspective, *He who loves community destroys community; he who loves the brethren builds community*, Vanier writes, "Community is not an ideal; it is people. It is you and I."[60] Hence, community as a place is more than an abstraction. It is the visible body of persons living out their fidelity to others in ways that cultivate time, space, and opportunity, leading to openness and acceptance of others.

Vanier's understanding of community as place also involves a theological dimension that has some similarity to what Martin Buber calls the "place of theophany," the notion that humanity encounters God via living out their fidelity to each other.[61] Vanier writes, "My fidelity to Jesus is also realized in my fidelity to my brother and sisters of L'Arche and especially the poorest."[62] In encountering the other one encounters God actively appearing within the story of human existence lending meaning to human existence and relatedness. For this reason, community as place emerges through encounters in which belonging, love and acceptance, caring, and growth in love regularly occur.[63]

---

57. Vanier, *Community and Growth*, 2.

58. Ibid.

59. Ibid., 10.

60. Vanier, *From Brokenness to Community*, 35.

61. Buber, *Between Man and Man*, 7. Buber writes, "We expect a theophany of which we know nothing but the place, and the place is called community."

62. Vanier, *Community and Growth*, 89.

63. Ibid., 8.

Underlying these theological impulses is Vanier's conviction that God creates humanity for the purpose of being, belonging, and living in community. Commenting on the purpose of creation within the Genesis account, Vanier writes, "In the beginning God made man and woman, so that they become one. Then we hear of how man and woman turned away from God because they wanted autonomy rather than to come together in God and with God."[64] Humanity's turning away from God, for Vanier, was a turning away from one of the fundamental reasons for which man and woman were created—being, belonging, and living in community. Not only do man and woman reject the divine creative purpose of communion with God but also relationship with one another. Insofar as turning away from God involves rejecting God's creative design for human existence, man and woman's rejection of God is an act of refusing to live out their full humanity. For this reason, a turning away from God is essentially a rejection of the other and self—all that is human.

Although Vanier does not employ *imago dei* language here, his reference to man and woman indicates that he at least perceives a linkage between the image of God and human sociality, or more precisely, male and female relatedness. In *Man and Woman God Made Them* Vanier's reading of human relationship as *imago dei* makes this linkage explicit. Vanier writes, "God created them [human beings] male and female, wanting them to be created to be a gift for each other . . . [E]ach in the image of God, they are called to become like God . . . [T]hey are also a reflection of the image of God in their union and their unity of love."[65] Viewed in this context, human relationship is an integral constituent of the dis-

64. Vanier, *Encountering 'the Other,'* 28.

65. Vanier, *Man and Woman God Made Them,* 49. This work was first published in 1984 in French under the title *Homme et Femme Il les Fit* and in English in 1985. Though it was revised in 2007, primarily to address the development and decadence of cultural perspectives on human sexuality, Vanier's understanding that relationship as the *imago dei* was present within the first edition. For this reason, I am reading the reference to "man and woman" in *Encountering 'the Other'* as an allusion to human sociality as *imago dei* within Vanier's theology of community

tinct nature of human creaturely existence. Vanier writes, "Such is their fundamental goal in the universe . . . [Relationship] is the goal of our unique createdness as we put our gifts and capacities at the service of others."[66] This occurs by way of human relatedness that takes God as its primary aim that male and female reflect the *imago dei* and discover their being in relation to God as well as his or her self in relation to the other.[67] Clearly, human relationship as *imago dei* plays a prominent role within Vanier's theology of community. Vanier understands human relationship as *imago dei* involving both the inherent uniqueness and relatedness between human beings. Both male and female are created in the *imago dei* as well as reflect the *imago dei* in their relation to one another.

Vanier's relational interpretation of *imago dei* presupposes other theological features fundamental to his understanding of God's nature in relation to community. In view of the foregoing analysis, one of God's communal purposes for creating man and woman is to become one so that "in their union and unity of love" man and woman reflect God. For this reason, human relationship reflects the unique social nature of God—"a community of being." Methodologically, Vanier appeals to the incarnation of Jesus from a redemptive historical perspective to draw out the divine purpose and linkage between human sociality and God's intrinsic social nature. Commenting on the divine activity of the *Logos* in the incarnation, Vanier writes, "The Gospel of John begins with an extraordinary poetic, mystical vision of the healing of humanity, which in some way condenses the history of salvation."[68] Correspondingly, "The Word became flesh and dwelt amongst us and then we see that the whole of the vision of Jesus is bringing people together," writes Vanier.[69] In this way God's eternal purposes and claim on creaturely existence are understood through Christ's work. Both communal and unifying dimensions of God's eternal purposes are realized in Christ Jesus from creation to redemption.

66. Ibid.

67. Ibid.

68. Vanier, *Drawn into the Mystery of Jesus*, 18.

69. Vanier, *Encountering 'the Other,'* 27–28.

Highlighting another divine purpose of Jesus' incarnation, Vanier writes:

> Jesus came to reveal to humanity that God is not a solitary, eternal being, contemplating his own glory . . . God is a family of three; three persons in communion one with another, giving themselves totally one to another, each one relative to the other. And God created man and woman as a sign of the Trinity; he created them to be in communion, one with the other, in this way reflecting his Love. God yearns for community to be a sign of this community between Father, Son and Holy Spirit.[70]

According to Vanier, the purpose of the incarnation involves Jesus revealing the particularity of the social nature within the Godhead. God is a family whose relations are self-giving. Vanier sees an analogical linkage between humanity's self-giving and God's internal life as self-giving. This linkage is evidenced in the language of man and woman being a sign of the Trinity, which lends theological support to Vanier's contention that God as a social being created self-conscious creatures with certain inherent social attributes constitutive of their distinct nature for the purpose to bear the sign of community that God is as Trinity.

Clearly, Vanier views the Trinity as a social model for community. Within his theology Vanier places emphasis on the linkage between solidarity and the communal exchange of divine life within the Godhead. Moreover, he understands the social exchange of divine life with divine life as reciprocally constituting divine solidarity within the Godhead.[71] God's desire for community, for

70. Vanier, *Community and Growth*, 59.

71. *Perichoresis* is the Greek word used to describe the social nature and triune relationship between each person of the Godhead. *Perichoresis* "allows the individuality of the persons to be maintained, while insisting that each person shares in the life of the other two. An image often used to express this idea is that of a 'community of being,' in which each person, while maintaining its distinctive identity, penetrates the others and is penetrated by them," writes McGrath. See McGrath, *Christian Theology*, 325. God's triune community of being is a "dynamic process of making room for another around oneself," writes Lawler. See Lawler, "Perichoresis," 49. As we will see, Vanier's relational interpretation of the *imago dei* is shaped by the embodied witness of L'Arche, a

Vanier, is to be a visible sign of solidarity and community between Father, Son, and Holy Spirit. On this account, Vanier interprets the Trinity not as a conceptual icon but as a way of life communicating a divine "Yes" to life and life together. The unifying and communal dimensions within the divine life of the Godhead, for Vanier, is both prototype and foundation for cultivating an ethos of community that takes human solidarity as its primary aim.

On the shape of solidarity within his theology of community Vanier's appeals to the encyclical *Sollicitudo Rei Socialis* in which John Paul II writes:

> Beyond human and natural bonds, already so close and strong, there is discerned in the light of faith a new model of the unity of the human race, which must ultimately inspire our solidarity. This supreme model of unity, which is a reflection of the intimate life of God, one God in three Persons, is what we Christians mean by the word communion.[72]

Viewed in this context, the intimate exchange of life of the three persons of the Trinity is the theological and ethical basis for solidarity within Vanier's theology of community. Solidarity involves unity, intimate exchange of life, and the mutually shared reception of the other's presence, communion. In all its forms solidarity is the product of the encounter that takes place within the soil of community.[73]

Contemporary society, to a degree, for Vanier, is the product of disintegration.[74] Thus, solidarity stands in contrast to the fragmentary spirit of contemporary society. Where solidarity has disappeared the "breakdown of confidence in community values" within society has given rise to vicious forms of individualism that shape the hierarchy of individual and societal values.[75] Contrastingly, community, for Vanier, has the capacity to cultivate an ethos

community that exists for the purpose of making room for others.

72. John Paul II, Encyclical Letter, *Sollicitudo Rei Socialis*, no. 40.

73. Vanier, *Community and Growth*, 165.

74. Ibid., 1–2.

75. Ibid.

of solidarity visibly expressed through gestures of mutual support, togetherness, and belonging. Here, it is important to note how solidarity, for Vanier, does not entail forms of uniformity, conformity, or sameness. Vanier's vision for community does not seek to set up a system of control that gives way to coercive conformity of persons. He recognizes the theological significance of identity and the corresponding entailments of individual uniqueness and particularity. He writes, "That is what a community is about—each person is seen as unique . . . Each one of us is very different from the other. But all together we are like a symphony, an orchestra . . . That means, however, that we must learn to love difference, to see it as a treasure and not as a threat."[76] Individual creaturely distinctiveness is not displaced but rather integrated into Vanier's vision and ethos of community. Solidarity is the product of community in which mutual respect, support, and love of individual uniqueness is valued. More so, it is in fidelity to both the vision and embodiment of solidarity that "we discover that the body [of persons] which is community is the place of communion."[77] Essentially, community is the soil in which solidarity and communion take root and spring into visible forms of unity, mutual respect, welcome, and love. Insofar as its soil provides the place and opportunity for cultivating human relatedness that lead to concrete expressions of solidarity, community is life giving and unifying.[78]

Underlying Vanier's understanding of the intrinsic life-giving and unifying nature of community is his theological belief that humans are created for community with and in God. As we have seen, man and woman, for Vanier, are created to be one body in relation to God who created them.[79] Not only were man and woman created for each other but also for sharing communion with and in the presence of God. Vanier believes that part of God's creative

76. Vanier, *From Brokenness to Community*, 43.

77. Ibid., 43–44.

78. The life-giving nature of community is a predominant theme throughout Vanier's writings. It is emphasized especially in Vanier, *Community and Growth*, 84–101, 165–203 and Vanier, *From Brokenness to Community*, 10.

79. Vanier, *Community and Growth*, 49.

plan for humanity involves participation with and in the life of God.[80] Reading the *imago dei* as the inherent impulse that propels humanity to seek communion, Vanier writes, "The thirst for union . . . in the depths of the human person is in the image of God who is absolute love and infinite fecundity."[81] Hence, the desire for communion with God and others is deeply embedded within our humanity.[82] More so, this communion can only be realized if it "receives power and strength from God and be marked by the divine qualities of fidelity and truth."[83] On this account, humanity is created for communion with God. And the God who creates humanity for this purpose is the source from and means by which this communion is made possible and realized. Not only does God create communion as an integral constituent of the distinct nature of our human creatureliness but also acts as divine agent. Though existing before creation God enters into the story of creaturely existence to initiate an encounter with humanity so that we might realize our true self in relation to divine life, primarily, and others. Given these particulars, the Other—God—as well as others in relation to the Other make human life possible.

Throughout Vanier's works God's divine agency and movement of encounter within the story of human existence is also read from the perspective of Christ's work and claim on creation. Once more, Vanier's christological reading of the Gospel of John provides further clarity on his understanding of the entailments of human creaturely participation and communion with God. Commenting on John 17, Vanier writes, "The Word became one of us to reveal the face and heart of God and to lead us all into a loving communion with the Father. His yearning, his prayer is that we all become one in him; each one different, each one unique, but together in unity to the glory of God."[84] Contextually, this passage narrates the continuation of Christ's downward descent into weak-

---

80. Vanier, *Man and Woman God Made Them*, 72.

81. Ibid., 109.

82. Ibid., 181

83. Ibid., 109.

84. Vanier, *Drawn into the Mystery of Jesus*, 290.

ness and death. Although his downward descent began with the incarnation, this particular passage follows closely behind Christ's washing of the disciples feet in which he willingly enters into a place of profound vulnerability and paradoxically reveals the very nature of God and a new way for humanity to paradoxically "exercise authority [in weakness] to bring people to unity" and communion with God.[85] Thus, Jesus' high priestly prayer in John 17 further emphasizes the consistent fluidity of the divine creative and redemptive purposes for humanity. Interpreting this prayer as a song of praise in which Christ prays to God that all of humanity will be unified together in communion with God as he is with and in the Father, Vanier writes, "Now, in this moment of contemplation, Jesus reveals . . . [that] it is no longer descending into flesh but the flesh of humanity ascending into God. It is no longer the Word who becomes a human being, but human beings transformed into God."[86] God's presence within the story of human existence is to provide the way into communion with God. Through communion with God human creatures discover the way of life for which they have been created—the way to be and become fully human. Vanier writes, "[Community is not] just to enter a group, or a tribe, but to become fully human in communion with God, that's what God wants, for 'the glory of God is people fully alive.'"[87]

Living in Community: A Living Body

At this point it is important to note that practically everything Vanier says concerning living in community stems from his experience of life in L'Arche, which is linked with the Christian religious tradition and the church.[88] For this reason, Vanier often describes community using a theological register that is comparable in certain respects to biblical and theological language

85. Ibid., 223.

86. Ibid., 290–92.

87. Vanier, *Encountering 'the Other,'* 41.

88. Vanier, *Community and Growth*, 11. Vanier states, "Everything I say about life in community in these pages is inspired by my faith in Jesus."

designated for the church. Although he does not claim or imply that every community in which persons live out their fidelity to/ for the other is a Christian community or that each person within these communities are necessarily Christian, Vanier does believe that all communities are comprised of persons who are called to belong to one another and to God. Vanier writes, "Each of us has been personally called to live together, to belong to the same community, the same body. This call is the foundation of our decision to commit ourselves with others for others, responsible for each other."[89] Drawing from the first epistle to the Corinthian church in which the biblical author identifies the church as a faithful body comprised of many different parts, Vanier writes, "Every community is a body, and in it all the members belong one to another."[90] Commenting on the *telos* of community, Vanier writes, "Community . . . is not an end in itself. It is people and love and communion with God that are the goal."[91] On this account, community is a way of life in which people are called by God to live in the presence of God in communion with others and God in order to be a sign of God's presence.[92]

Community is the concretization of humanity's yearning for God in which liberation and growth are given definite shape in and through gestures of welcome, encounter, love, trust, and forgiveness of the other.[93] More so, that which makes community possible is "when people start truly caring for each other and for each other's growth," writes Vanier.[94] Here, Vanier emphasizes the significance of how care and growth for others are fundamental

---

89. Vanier, *Encountering the 'Other,'* 49.

90. Vanier, *Community and Growth*, 49.

91. Ibid., 22.

92. These notions of community as a way of life, calling, communion, and being a sign of God's presence can be found in Vanier, *Community and Growth*, 11, 16, 25, 30, 44–47, 68, 84–85, 92–93, 131–34, 157. Also, see Vanier, *Man and Woman God Made Them*, 175.

93. Vanier, *Community and Growth*, 16, 30, 93, 131–34.

94. Ibid., 20.

constituents of the distinct nature of genuine community.[95] Both caring and growth, for Vanier, are signs of a life-giving community. Vanier writes, "Community must never take precedence over individual people. It is for people and for their growth."[96] Community is a place of growth; it is life-giving. In the light of Vanier's emphasis on caring for each other and each others growth, what makes community possible is exactly the fact of persons living out their fidelity for one another by way of being present-*for* the other in a life giving manner.[97]

Assessment

In this chapter we have analyzed particular impulses and features that underlie, influence, and play a central role in Vanier's thinking on community. Vanier sees community as an inherent feature of God's creative purposes for humanity. Humanity has been created for sharing communion with one another as well as with and in the presence of God. Hence, community is an essential characteristic of our human nature and creaturely existence. Vanier reads humanity's rejection of God in Adam's fall as a turning away from God's creative design for creaturely existence. In rejecting God humanity abandons what it means to be and become fully human, that is, being, belonging, and living in community.

The assessment of solidarity clarifies how contemporary society, for Vanier, is a product of fragmentation rooted in humanity's search for self-autonomy. Unity, solidarity, and community

95. Ibid., 10. See Vanier, *From Brokenness to Community*, 35.

96. Ibid., 21.

97. In the light of the foregoing development of what being present-*for* the other does and does not entail combined with the ways in which I have located this grammar within particular contexts of listening and living out one's fidelity to the other—phenomena that presuppose being, belonging, presence, and "living together"—it is my contention that Vanier's understanding of how caring for others makes community possible does not displace any emphasis on living together and/or the significance of the attempt to understand our own vulnerability as key elements to community, in general, and, in particular, L'Arche.

stand in opposition to the individualistic spirit that shapes what Vanier sees as the hierarchy of individual and societal values. Even though these powers and principalities are at work within society, Vanier maintains that the desire for communion with others and union with God is inextricably embedded within our humanity. Moreover, the *imago dei* engenders human desire for communion with otherness. For this reason, living in community and fulfilling what it means to be and become fully human can be made a reality. As we have seen, Christ's entering the story of human existence to initiate an encounter with humanity so that we might become fully conscious of our true self in relation to God and others, for Vanier, is necessary. This chapter has brought to light how Vanier's reading Christ's claim on creation, vision for humanity, and reconciliatory work in relation to one another further clarifies his understanding of God's creative and redemptive purposes for creaturely life— participation and communion with God and others. For Vanier, Christ makes known God's creative purposes for humanity by providing a way into communion with God and others within the story of human existence. Through encountering God's presence in the world we discover how to be and become fully human.

Vanier believes that community engenders encounters in which time, space, and opportunity are given for human growth. Through encountering others we encounter reality as it is revealed and given. Because Vanier sees reality as the first principle of truth, being and becoming fully human involves remaining connected to reality.[98] This requires that we begin to unmask the illusions, dreams, fantasy, and fears of our selected and modified realities that close us in on ourselves and begin to accept ourselves just as we are and others as they are. Moreover, this phenomenon presupposes that welcoming reality as it *is* occurs through encountering others, not in isolation. On this account, community, for Vanier, is a place in which we discover who we are in relation to the other.

Another particular that has emerged in this chapter is Vanier's account of the ways in which the most vulnerable persons in

98. Reinders describes Vanier's primary concern with the reality of life in terms of "theological realism." See Reinders, "Being with the Disabled."

society are sources of life, communion, and unity *intus et extra ecclesiae*. According to Vanier, the weak and the poor are visible expressions of the God's pneumatological reality within the church and Christ's presence within the world. Thus, communion with the vulnerable, for Vanier, is communion with God.

At a deeper level the distinctive attributes that characterize the communal ethos within Vanier's writings and L'Arche facilitate the necessary conversation about what it means to be human. Taking God to be the primary object from which community originates, Vanier conveys the notion that living humanly involves both an awareness of and responsiveness to God's activity in the story of human existence. Thus, the synthetic details of the foregoing account call attention to humanity's need to remain responsive to the God who appears in and through the other, especially those who are considered the least of these *intus et extra ecclesiae*.

4

Welcome as a Way of Life
within Community

THIS CHAPTER DRAWS ATTENTION to Vanier's theological conviction that Christ's presence is realized within the ordinary composition of daily life with the hope to bring to light the relevancy of how Christ's presence concretized in others, especially vulnerable persons, gives shape to what it means to be present-*for* others, and thus calls into question how society has come to understand and behave toward conditions of human limitation. It is my contention that Vanier's communal account carries with it a theology of care that raises conceptual questions about the values accorded to the self and the distinctive qualities that are often regarded as holding personhood, identity, and individuality in place within society. For this reason, this chapter examines the practice of care provision within L'Arche, which I believe provides a lens by which we can theologically distinguish what forms of care and treatment are humane from those that depersonalize and objectify persons. The final section of this chapter returns to Vanier's understanding of what roots of community, what attitudes inform ways of life in community, and what breaks down community in terms of what I propose to name as "faithful exploration" in remaining responsive to the presence of God within the course of life. By way of drawing attention to the emphasis Vanier places on God's ways with humanity in the course of life, the purpose of this final chapter of the book is to demonstrate how Vanier's account provides a platform for Christian ethics to explore ways of speaking about God.

On Listening and Being Human

THE PLACE AND ROLE of listening and remaining responsive to God and, in particular, God's activity within the story of human existence within the shaping of Christian ethos, is central to Vanier's practical theology. Because the nature of listening and remaining responsive to God's divine action, for Vanier, are central constituents of the distinct nature of what it means to be and become human, his account of community facilitates the necessary conversations about the story of human life in which God becomes active in creation through the activity of God's Word as well as how we encounter, listen, and remain responsive to God's Word and divine action and presence. To a considerable extent Vanier sees God, as God is encounter, as the focal point of Christian ethics. According to Vanier, Christian ethics involves inquiring into and speaking about God, God's encountering humanity, self-conscious creaturely attentiveness to God, and the ways in which humanity welcomes the divine encounter by way of joining in participation with the God whose perfect will is the object of theological and ethical inquiry.

It is important to note how Vanier's personal trajectory embodies the epistemology inherent to his account; that is to say, that human wholeness lies in listening and remaining responsive to God's will and activity within the world. As previously mentioned, the advent of Vanier and L'Arche occurred at a time in which global tensions and anxiety were forcing societies into competing modes of existence. On the whole, a characteristic spirit of despair, despondency, and fear dominated the culture in which Vanier emerged. Despite prevailing failing institutions and cultural conditions, Vanier received the challenge of the gospel with zealousness, strove for an unyielding obedience to the word and spirit of the gospel, and sought to respond to it with his whole life. Vanier's transition from a place of prestige and power to L'Arche is a personal account of a life lived in faithful exploration of God's will. Vanier's life is a visible expression of how listening and responsiveness is necessary for discerning the presence of God's activity within the story of human existence and putting into effect the word of the gospel. Like faith, which comes by way of hearing, and hearing from the word of God, L'Arche has its origin in God's address to Vanier. On this account, the trajectories of Vanier's life is analogous in character to the epistemology inherent to his communal account regarding L'Arche; an epistemology in which human wholeness is understood to lie in listening and remaining responsive to God's will and activity within the world.

Humanity, according to Vanier, receives its nature. "Man has not created it himself. If, therefore, we are to attain fullness of life, it is a matter of listening to this nature."[1] "We did not ask to be born. We do not know when or how we will die. We do not possess life. We received it," writes Vanier.[2] Being human, for Vanier, is about becoming human by means of accepting the state of life; that is to say, the truth of reality given as gift. Vanier sees what it means to be human as "becoming" human. Vanier locates what it means to be human within an active register involving human activity in which human beings grow in their humanity, becoming fully human.[3] Consequently, Vanier's account of what it means to be human carries with it certain ontological beliefs that are

1. Vanier, *Made for Happiness*, 193.

2. Vanier, "What Have People with Learning Disabilities Taught Me?," 23.

3. "Becoming" human is a monolithic theme running in the foreground of Vanier's works. See Vanier, *Made for Happiness*, 43, 143; Vanier, *Our Journey Home*, 137–72; and Vanier, *Becoming Human*.

comparable to a degree to a Thomistic understanding of "being is activity."[4] By way of locating "being" human within a register of "becoming" human, Vanier's account raises questions about the conceptual grammar pertaining to metaphysical discourse centered on ontological distinctions between "being" and "doing" as if these phenomena are mutually exclusive realities.

Accordingly, the reality of life, for Vanier, is a first principle.[5] Moreover, being as becoming human involves a way of life that is inclined to listening and remaining responsive to the truth of reality as it *is* with all is complexities and beauty. It entails "accepting and choosing life, not just submitting grudgingly to it. It comes when we choose to be who we are, to be ourselves, at this present moment of our lives; we choose life as it is, with all its joys, pain, and conflicts," writes Vanier.[6] Commenting on the ways in which human wholeness lay in becoming present to the truth of reality, Vanier writes:

> Happiness is living and seeking truth, together with others in community, and assuming responsibility for our lives and the lives of others. It is accepting the fact that we are not infinite . . . We are not just seeking to be what others want us to be or to conform to the expectations of family, friends, or local ways of being. We have chosen to be who we are, with all that is beautiful and broken in us. We do not slip away from life . . . We become present to reality and to life so that we are free to live.[7]

Becoming present to reality and to life involves an ethos of listening and responsiveness to the reality of the givenness of one's humanity. This phenomenon is intrinsic to reality; thus, the capacity to listen and remain responsive to the truth of reality emerges

---

4. Hauerwas, "Seeing Peace," 120n12; and Burrell, *Aquinas,* 45–48.

5. Vanier, *Becoming Human,* 114.

6. Vanier, *Finding Peace,* 54.

7. Ibid., 54–55. Contextually, Vanier locates "happiness" within a "finding peace" register that is similar in character and form to the Hebrew understanding of peace, *shalom;* that is, a form of peace in the midst of given constraints related to the reality of life as well as to "happiness" as desire for "fullness of life" and/or "wholeness."

from outside of oneself. At this point it is important to note that the ultimate foundation for human existence, according to Vanier, is Jesus Christ.[8] Humanity receives its nature from Christ. The Other to whom humanity belongs is God. The reality of life as it *is* originates in God—the Infinite reality "that we are not" and the truth Jesus came into the world in order to give witness to (John 19:37–38).[9] "Truth is what we see and touch and experience. It is not something we invent, but something we humbly receive and welcome, something that is bigger, greater than ourselves. But truth is often hidden from us, which is why it takes time and the help of others to discern truth," writes Vanier.[10] On this account, the reality of daily life is the forum for listening and remaining responsive to the constant form of God's call and activity within the story of human existence. Hence, the existential question undergirding Vanier's theological understanding of reality is, "How do I listen and remain responsive to God becoming and remaining present to me within the reality of human life"?

Though "becoming" human entails a way of seeking fullness of life, it is important not to overlook the fact that Vanier describes this explorative phenomenon in terms of one's perceptive awareness, or more precisely, "becoming present," to the dynamic of faith within all reality in all times and places. Hence, what it means to be human is to faithfully accept the givenness of reality as God's divine activity and grace within one's life. Reflecting upon the beginnings of L'Arche, Vanier situates this dynamic of faith within all reality as being "open to providence and daily life."[11] Vanier's

---

8. Vanier, *Living Gently in a Violent World*, 39.

9. Vanier, *Drawn into the Mystery of Jesus*, 160–61.

10. Ibid.

11. Vanier, *An Ark for the Poor*, 22. It is Vanier's meditative description of this dynamic of faith that has given shape to Hauerwas's Wittgensteinian interpretation of L'Arche in which he contends that L'Arche and Vanier, on the whole, embody a moral epistemology. See Hauerwas, "Seeing Peace," 117–18. Employing this hermeneutical lens, Reinders sees L'Arche emerging from Vanier's "deep awareness" and responsiveness to the dynamic of faith within the realities of life. "To attend to daily affairs and to look out for what came his way was a call of faith . . . God was working through the reality of [life]," writes

understanding of these matters exemplifies the central conviction that Christ's presence is realized within the ordinary composition of daily life.[12] Therefore, responding to the reality of life is responsiveness to God's activity within the story of human existence. As we accept and welcome the reality of who we are and others as they are we concretize our attentiveness and responsiveness to the divine purposes related to humanity and thus live out what it means to be and become human. As we have seen, this phenomenon, for Vanier, can take on many forms; it occurs in encountering and welcoming others and the reality of oneself as it *is* and, in particular, in a life shared in community with those who are most vulnerable within society and the church.

Vanier's account takes God as the fundamental truth underlying all reality. As a result, the life to which humanity is called is a life in the presence of God within the present moment of one's reality. Since God is the primary reality that gives shape to the state of all things as they actually exist, then listening and remaining responsive to reality, for Vanier, is to listen and remain responsive to God, the One who is creator, means, and goal of all revealed and

---

Reinders. See Reinders "Being with the Disabled," 470–71.

12. Though it lies beyond the scope of this chapter, it seems clear to me that Vanier's insistence on "becoming" present to the state of things as they actually exist combined with his understanding of the truth of the reality of life and the nature of man gives form to the idea put forth by Hauerwas concerning "Vanier's understanding of these matters with regard to the debates occasioned by de Lubac's understanding of the relationship of nature and grace." It is my contention that Vanier's emphasis on how "becoming" present to the dynamic of faith within the realities of life in all times and places constitutes what it means *to be human* exemplifies de Lubac's belief that grace is not extrinsically related to nature and that the state of things as they actually exist possess a sacramental character capable of drawing humanity into a deeper participation in the presence of God within all created existence. See Hauerwas, "Seeing Peace," 123n15. For more information on the discourse related to how de Lubac's sacramental ontology calls into question what is universally perceived as the regnant neo-Thomist separation between nature and the supernatural, see Milbank, *The Suspended Middle*; von Balthasar, *The Theology of Henri de Lubac*; Komonchak, "Theology and Culture at Mid-Century"; Doyle "Henri de Lubac and the Roots of Communion Ecclesiology"; and Rowland, *Culture and the Thomist Tradition after Vatican II*.

given reality. Therefore, what it means to be and become human, for Vanier, is essentially reponsivity to God's divine address, activity, and presence within reality.

According to Vanier, listening and responsiveness to God is realized within time and space. Vanier's account draws attention to a way of life in which opportunity within time and space is given for listening and responsiveness to God and others. What is being implied here is that being addressed by God, for Vanier, is an integral constituent of the distinctive nature of what it means to be human. God's address to man, or more precisely, "God as God is encounter," is the indispensable quality that determines how man and woman ought to live, thus forming the moral life of the human creature. Therefore, listening and remaining responsive to the divine address is essential to what it means to be human. By way of listening and remaining responsive to God human beings affirm the fact of being whom and for which they are created and redeemed. For this reason, being and becoming human entails attending to the present moment within the quotidian fabric of life whether at work, washing dishes, in serving others, caring for the vulnerable, welcoming the guest, or befriending the stranger.[13] It is precisely in the present encounter, in accepting and responding to the reality of one's circumstances that we live out what it means to be and become human in the presence of the One who is creator, means, and goal of all revealed and given reality.

Vanier's understanding of what it means to be human raises conceptual questions about the prevailing cultural assumptions that give the individuating self a predominate place within contemporary culture, praise self-validating intuitions, and suggest that autonomy is the key to holding personhood, identity, and individuality in place within our contemporary forms of life. Vanier sees God as the source from which all reality exists and experience flows. Taking God as his primary aim, Vanier agrees that humanity

---

13. Here I am in conversation with Mark O'Keefe on the ways in which the "present moment" and "present encounter" relate to living the Christian life in God's presence. See O'Keefe, "The Unity of Christian Morality and Spirituality," 7–9.

belongs wholly to God, that the other—God, primarily, and others—constitute one's true self, holding personhood, identity, and individuality in place. Fullness of life emerges in relatedness to others not from one's own capacity to fulfill their self by way of utilizing reason and/or working in an efficient and effective manner. Contrary to the rationalist reduction of the self and the cultural assumptions that regard rationality and autonomy as constitutive qualities necessary for holding personhood, identity, and individuality in place, Vanier sees humanity discovering its true self in relation to Christ within the story of our human lives and others. Thus, relatedness to others is the way to the fullness of our humanity. It is because of Christ's possession of our humanity that personhood, identity, and individuality, for Vanier, are fundamentally constituted in relatedness to Christ, primarily, and others. Dependency, or more precisely, "the other" constitutes one's self, not rationality and/or autonomy.

Clearly, Vanier's account of community narrates an account of the activity and presence of God's Word within the course of creaturely life and how self-conscious creatures listen and remain responsive to God's Word and divine action and presence in the world. Nevertheless, his account possesses a distinct way of naming the constant form of God's activity and presence within the quotidian fabric of life to which humanity attends. As we will see, Vanier emphasizes being in communion with others, especially with those who are vulnerable within society, not only as the visible expression of one's listening and responsiveness to the constant form of the divine presence and activity of God within the world in the course of life but also the concretization of what it means to be and become truly human.

The presence of Christ and caring *for* others

Throughout the foregoing chapters we have examined the ways in which different individuals, according to Vanier, convey the specificity of Christ's claim on humanity. Vanier sees the reality of life as offering an array of conduits for encountering God; all of life takes place in the presence of God, theologically speaking. For this reason, life is given to faithful listening and responsiveness to God's active Word within ordinary time and space in which we faithfully explore God's will, participating with God and others in living the Christian moral life in God's presence. Because Christ is present the moral task is to attend to the present moment.[14]

Vanier's account of community narrates a way of life in which presence of and communion with others are integral to what it means to be human. Vanier writes, "The world of presence and communion is an integral part of our being."[15] On the whole, his communal account calls us to accept that which is fundamental to our creaturely existence, namely, that the other—God, primarily, and others—lay claim to our being; and thus, constitute our true self. When moral existence is restored to its place in Christ, being and becoming human involves expressing one's true self in living out one's fidelity to the commonly held vision that others lay claim to one's being by way of being present-*for* others. For Vanier, this relational dynamic is, in essence, a belonging that is given shape in listening and responsiveness to the cries of those who are vulnerable, weak, and poor through gestures of welcoming others, befriending the stranger, and celebrating difference; gestures that hold the capacity for crossing barriers among and within us so that we might become fully human. Because vulnerability, weakness, and poverty are not limited to persons with disabilities or those who visibly show weakness but rather are integral to human nature, these gestures, for Vanier, are neither unilateral in nature nor exclusive activities of carers as benefactors.[16]

Though existing in many forms this relational dynamic involves attending to the present moment with the intention to faithfully explore given opportunities within time and space to encounter God's active presence within the story of human existence. Moreover, to be present-*for* the other is to be present-*for* Christ.

14. Ibid., 7–9.

15. Vanier, *Eruption to Hope*, 24.

16. The notion of vulnerability being an integral constituent of our common humanity is a predominant theme in Vanier's *Becoming Human*.

Being present-*for* others is a way of concretizing one's listening and responsiveness to God's active presence within creation. Not only does Christ's presence give shape to what it means to be present-*for* others but also to the ways in which this relational dynamic is carried out within the context of caring for others.

"Jesus tells us that he is hidden in the face of the poor, that he is in fact poor . . . [T]he smallest gesture of love towards the least significant person is a gesture of love towards him. Jesus is . . . the sick, the dying, the oppressed, the humiliated," writes Vanier.[17] Hence, caring for the other originates from a Christocentric perspective that gives shape to the perception of Christ's presence in the other, the value of caring for the other, and the manner in which caring is rendered. Christ's presence within the other revalues and reorients the ways in which caring for others occur. Each person ought to be approached out of honor and with respect. According to Vanier, "People who gather together to live the presence of Jesus among people in distress are therefore called not just to do things for them, or to see them as objects of charity, but rather to receive them as a source of life and communion."[18] Though they possess needs and wounds that demand, to a degree, liberation and healing, they are—because of their needs and wounds—sources of liberation and healing.[19] Paradoxically, those whom society considers as lacking fullness of life are sources of life. Moreover, those whom society marginalize, institutionalize, hospitalize, and consign to places of isolation are sources of communion.[20] For this reason, to

17. Vanier, *Community and Growth*, 95.

18. Ibid.

19. Ibid, 96.

20. Here, I am simply drawing attention to how persons in isolation, theologically speaking, paradoxically are sources of communion. Therefore, the purpose of this critique is not to question whether or not sick and/or injured persons ought to be admitted to institutions for medical and surgical treatment and/or nursing care. However, subsequent reflection will raise conceptual questions concerning the societal impulses that drive the institutionalization of persons because they are hard to deal with and/or in the light of perceived needs to cure, heal, and liberate what is merely symptomatic while simultaneously denying what it means to be and become human.

be present with the poor, the sick, vulnerable, and distressed is to care and be present with Jesus and vice versa.[21] By way of placing Christ at the center of all caring operations Vanier identifies how caring has an inherent relationship to the way in which persons worship. Caring for others is a means by which persons visibly express their faith in and worship of God, or more precisely, one's responsiveness to God's divine action via the inbreaking of the presence of Christ who claims the carer, sick, poor, and vulnerable. At this point it is important to note that Christ's presence is not a mere abstraction. Vanier writes, "The smallest gesture of love towards the least significant person is a gesture of love towards him [Jesus]."[22] Hence, Vanier sees the real presence of Jesus in the poor; to care for them is to care for Christ. What is being implied here is that Christ's presence is not a static presence that is worshiped. Moreover, this is not an ideological declaration about Christ's real presence in the vulnerable but instead a matter of when we care for others, we care for Christ.

Seeing Christ's present within those who are in need of care cultivates forms of listening and responsiveness in which mutual love, respect, and service free from all pretense, deceit, and self-projection can occur between carers and those who are cared for. At the same time it protects carers from objectifying persons who are in need of care in a way that degrades persons as well as safeguards those in need of care against technical and impersonal forms of carelessness. At a deeper level, caring that is carried out in this manner calls into question therapeutic (everything can be treated), technological (everything can be fixed), and consumerist (what one wants, one can get)[23] impulses that underlie and give shape to the way human society has come to understand health, care, humanity, and the good. In what follows, an overview of the

21. Ibid., 95.

22. Ibid.

23. Here I am in conversation with Raymond Studzinski, Nicholas Wolterstorff, and Walter Brueggemann on theological perspectives of cultural scripts. See Brueggemann, "Counterscript," 22–23; Studzinski, *Reading to Live*, 209; and Wolterstorff, "Living Within a Text," 212.

ways in which human society understands and behaves toward conditions of human limitation, a constructive theological analysis of care within L'Arche, and a detailed discussion on thematic features related to caring within Vanier's writings will be given in order to demonstrate how Vanier's account provides a lens by which we can theologically distinguish what forms of care and treatment are humane from those that depersonalize and objectify persons.

Human Societal Perception(s) of Human Limitation

On the whole, human society is driven by "the selfish use of other persons, the desire to have more than is necessary, the manipulation of others for one's own advantage, . . . [the drive] to have as much pleasure as possible, to abuse privileges and deceive others."[24] We seek flight from difficult situations, especially in relation to human limitation, vulnerability, and sickness. It is for society to come to terms with the limits of humanity. The limits of suffering, weakness, dependence, and vulnerability are at variance with our culture. In fact, the limits of humanity are not only problematic for those experiencing certain limits but also for those who care for them. This is evidenced by how human society perceives and acts toward persons who lack strength and/or possess features regarded as a disadvantage or fault. Rather than accepting human life as "a mystery of growth from weakness to weakness, from the weakness of the little baby to the weakness of the aged" human society lives under the illusion that everything can and will be treated, cured, and fixed.[25] But when faced with the truth of reality of profound limits that result in contrastive outcomes, contemporary society responds in a way paralleling third-century pagan reaction to weakness, sickness, and the dying. "They deserted those who began to be sick, and fled from their dearest friends.

24. Roberts, *Centered on Christ*, 94.
25. Vanier, *Becoming Human*, 39.

And they cast them out into the streets when they were half dead, and left the dead like refuse, unburied. They shunned any participation or fellowship with death."[26] In general, we hospitalize the sick, consign the elderly to nursing homes, confine the dying to places of isolation, and ward off persons with disabilities and mental impairments to institutions despite prevailing circumstances that might result in a lack of better or humane care/treatment, all because these persons are, in view of the type of product society seeks to produce, too difficult to cope with. Böckmann writes, "Not all organizations guarantee fully human care that respects the true dignity of the sick. How quickly are the aged and sick treated like infant and numbers!"[27] For this reason, the ways we have come to understand and act toward sickness, vulnerability, and human limitation epitomize how human society denies the relevance of vulnerability as an integral constituent of the distinct nature of what it means to be and become human. To refuse to admit that human life is limited, suggests Vanier, is to deny death; it is a denial of that which is a fundamental part of what it means to be human.[28] "Weakness speaks to us of the ultimate powerlessness, of death itself. To be small, to be sick, to be dying, to be dead, are stages of powerlessness, they appear to us to be anti-life and so we deny them."[29] When we repudiate those constraints that limit and render us powerless we not only deny certain conditions associated with humanity but also the value of being individual persons. Paradoxically, in denying what we perceive as being anti-life we essentially deny the truth of reality, and thus deny what it means to be and become fully human, given constraints.

26. Eusebius, *Church History*, Nicene and Post-Nicene Fathers, 307.

27. Böckmann, *Growing in Mutual Service and* Love, 130.

28. Vanier, *Becoming Human*, 40.

29. Ibid.

Care within L'Arche

L'Arche originated from his listening to the cry of the poor—persons with disabilities, Vanier writes:

> This cry, "Do you love me? Am I important? Will you be my friend?" was expressed or written on the faces of those men and of many others in different institutions and of those living in painful situations. I wanted to create a place where they could find inner freedom, develop their personhood and abilities, and be fulfilled, where they could let their deepest desires rise up and find a new meaning for their lives.[30]

As a result, "The aim of L'Arche is to create communities, which welcome people with a mental handicap. By this means, L'Arche seeks to respond to the distress of those who are too often rejected, and to give them a valid place in society."[31] On this account, listening underlies and informs the ways in which caring for persons with disabilities take shape in L'Arche. Commenting on how listening shapes caring within L'Arche, Vanier writes:

> I discovered that to love people is not first of all to do things for them but to reveal something to them. It is to reveal that they have a value, that they are beautiful and precious, that there is meaning to their lives . . . This is done through our being with them, enjoying their presence, listening to them, understanding their pain and their needs, becoming their friend and being vulnerable to them.[32]

30. Vanier, "What Have People with Learning Disabilities Taught Me?," 20.

31. Vanier, *An Ark for the Poor*, 148.

32. Vanier, "L'Arche—A Place of Communion and Pain," 16–17. At this point it is important to note that the preceding development of being present-*for* others in need of care is not the same as doing things for persons in need of care. In the light of the foregoing sections in this book being present-*for* others involves attitudes and expressions analogous to the relational characteristics Vanier highlights above. In other words, being present-*for* others characterizes the whole economy of living and being with others within Vanier's writings and L'Arche.

Revealing to another their unique value and beauty is a way of expressing one's love for another. This phenomenon supposes time, opportunity, and space for listening, attentiveness, and genuine responsiveness. Vanier writes, "To reveal someone's beauty is to reveal their value by giving them time, attention, and tenderness . . . We can express this revelation through our open and gentle presence, in the way we look at and listen to a person, the way we speak to and care for someone."[33] At this point it is important to note that even though Vanier explicitly employs the grammar "being with" rather than "being present-*for* another," he contextually locates this language alongside "enjoying their presence, listening to them," and "becoming their friend." Therefore, "being with" others, according to Vanier, does not give the impression of an insignificant physical presence or having nothing to do with friendship. Neither does it suggest being present "to" another, which often involves coveting to possess all one can from the other.[34] By way of situating "being with" within a larger discourse concerning the ways in which love is concretized in and through friendship, presence, listening, and understanding, Vanier gives definite form to what it means to be present-*for* another within a context of caring. Vanier's understanding of care exemplifies that love of Aristotle that possesses the character of benevolent friendship, which seeks the good, well-being, and benefit of the other as its primary purpose. According to Aristotle, a friend is "one who wishes and does what is good, or seems so, for the sake of the friend."[35] Correspondingly, Vanier writes, "In true friendship, everything, will and feelings alike, is oriented by this concern for the other person."[36] Friendship supposes a timefullness of sharing, life together, and communion with others.[37] Though it may seem like a moot point, the preposition "in" vis-à-vis "true friendship" sheds light on how time is an integral constituent of

33. Vanier, *Becoming Human*, 22.

34. O'Regan, "Listening," 556.

35. Aristotle, *Nicomachaen Ethics*, 1166a3–5

36. Vanier, *Made for Happiness*, 54–75, esp. 66.

37. Ibid., 55.

genuine friendship. Friendship is not a matter of course nor is it something automatic. Instead, it follows from the fruit of mutual belonging and "meaningful, authentic, respectful, and committed relationships" in space and time within a communal milieu.[38] Note the emphasis on the reciprocal nature of relational activity within Vanier's understanding of friendship. Vanier writes, "Friendship is primarily a life together that is nourished by shared activity and not by dreams about the other person."[39] On this account, "true friendship," for Vanier, moves beyond abstraction. As we will see, "true friendship," according to Vanier, underlies and influences the whole economy of care provision within L'Arche. Hence, care provision within L'Arche, as conveyed in Vanier's writings, involves a genuine covenant-like friendship, love, and wholehearted devotion to the good and growth of the other. On this account, "true friendship" is another way of naming care rooted in love oriented toward helping persons discover and welcome their true self. In this regard "true friendship," like love, is as vital as food for being and becoming fully human.[40]

In *Becoming Human* Vanier tells us about Claudia, a seven-year-old girl who had spent practically her entire life in a dismal, overcrowded asylum.[41] "Claudia was blind, fearful of relationships, filled with inner pain and anguish. Technically speaking she was autistic," Vanier explains.[42] Moreover, her departure from the asylum with all its "reference points, as well as the structured existence that had given her a certain security" further exacerbated her anguish upon her arrival at L'Arche.[43] "Everything and everyone frightened her; she screamed day and night and smeared excrement on the walls. She seemed totally mad; overwhelmed by insecurity, her personality appeared to be disintegrating," writes

38. Vanier, "What Have People with Learning Disabilities Taught Me?," 20–21. See Vanier, *Made for Happiness*, 54.

39. Ibid., 59.

40. Vanier, *Becoming Human*, 19.

41. Ibid., 20–33.

42. Ibid., 20.

43. Ibid., 21.

Vanier. "Claudia lived a horrible form of madness which should not be idealized or seen as a gateway to another world."[44] Vanier continues:

> In L'Arche, we have learned from our own experience of healing, as well as through the help of psychiatrists and psychologists, that chaos, or "madness," has meaning; it comes from somewhere, it is comprehensible. Madness is an immense cry, a sickness. It is a way of escaping when the stress of being in a world of pain is too great . . . But there is an order in the disorder that can permit healing, if only it can be found.[45]

Discovering the order that permits healing and growth is essential to caring for others in L'Arche. For Claudia, this discovery took many years. Seven years of isolation, loneliness, lack of love, and feelings of worthlessness in an asylum shaped the ways in which Claudia had come to understand and behave toward herself. Vanier explains, "Claudia had developed survival tactics and habits founded upon her belief in her own unworthiness. Her madness and screaming were reasonable responses to a world in which nobody wanted her. It took time for the transformation, from a hatred of herself to a trust in herself, to take place."[46] Once Claudia began to realize and discover she was loved, valuable, and unique her transformational journey from chaos, self-hate, and madness to inner peace and self-trust began.[47] Moreover, Claudia's discovery of her true self occurred by way of others welcoming, listening, understanding, and being present-*for* her; others made known to her that she was valuable, beautiful, unique, and a sacred gift to both her L'Arche community as well as the body of humanity. Twenty years after Claudia first arrived to L'Arche, Vanier recounts, "She was by then a twenty-eight–year-old woman, still blind and autistic but at peace and able to do many things in the community. She still likes being alone but she was clearly not a lonely person.

44. Ibid.
45. Ibid.
46. Ibid., 23.
47. Ibid., 22.

She would often sing to herself and there was a constant smile on her face."[48] Although she would experience anger on occasion, especially when she encountered a lack of respect or state of affairs that stimulated self-doubt and insecurity, Claudia was in good health.[49]

An important implication of Vanier's understanding of Claudia's well-being comes to the fore, namely, that "health" is understood and measured in ways contrary to cultural assumptions that calculate well being in terms of ability. Claudia's health, for Vanier, is measured in terms of her becoming aware that she was loved. Love is as vital as food for being and becoming fully human, Vanier explains.[50] "Each person, whatever his or her abilities or disabilities, needs to be nurtured in love. The desire to be loved as a person, as someone unique, is at the source of the person's development and at the source of all self-esteem . . . In order to grow to greater fulfillment, [persons] need a place of belonging where they feel loved and respected."[51] This growth supposes inclusion within community, the place in which one experiences mutual belonging, openness, vulnerability, presence, listening, understanding, love and caring; all of which played a role in revealing to Claudia that she was loved and could love others. Instead of calculating her health in relation to her capacity to be autonomous, ability to carefully plan and execute the navigation of her body within time and space or her possession of mental and physical power and agency, Vanier measures Claudia's wholeness and health in relation to her acceptance and welcome of the reality of her true self.[52] Essentially,

48. Ibid., 20.

49. Ibid., 21.

50. Ibid., 19.

51. Vanier, "What Have People with Learning Disabilities Taught Me?," 20.

52. Here I am in conversation with Reynolds, *Vulnerable Communion*, 65–67. Commenting on Mary Douglas's analysis of the morally charged cultural assumptions of taboo, "those things that are to be avoided because they challenge the conventions of a framework of valuation," Reynolds writes, "Human ability is understood and measured socially vis-à-vis an ideal moral condition . . . Ability means having power to move with conventions, to conform, to be

the notion of accepting the reality of one's self should be read in the light of the mission and aims of L'Arche to welcome persons with disabilities to help them discover their beauty and the meaning of their lives. According to Vanier, "This is done through our love and compassion; by meeting them where they are, in a heart-to-heart relationship"; by way of helping others stand on their own feet, trust in themselves and their own inner capacity for love.[53] Although Claudia possessed and experienced profound anguish, physical, and mental limitations resulting from blindness, autism, and other symptomatic conditions as well as the environmental surroundings in which she was placed, the revelation that she was valuable to others combined with her discovery of her own value, uniqueness, and sacredness, for Vanier and L'Arche, meant that she was in good health.[54]

Although Vanier acknowledges the technical description of the prevailing symptoms associated with Claudia's autism, neither the autism nor any other physical and/or mental impairments became the primary subject(s) of the care she received. That is to say, Claudia's medical needs did not primarily drive the type of care she received in L'Arche; her wholeness and health were not dependent upon the successful treatment of her autism, curing her blindness or the effective implementation of modifying behaviors, emotions, and/or a daily schedule. On this account, Vanier sees health as something other than curing or the state of being free from physical, mental, emotional, and psychological impairment, illness, and/or injury. It is vital to note that I am not denying L'Arche the recourse of technically addressing the real physical, emotional, behavioral, psychological, or neurasthenic conditions that originated from Claudia's disabilities. Nor am I suggesting L'Arche turned a blind eye to the medical-care need(s) of professional assistance made necessary by Claudia's impairments. Not

---

normal and whole, even to be holy. It means to control one's body in a certain way. How a community understands power and the good, therefore, has everything to do with how that community understands and responds to disability."

53. Vanier, *The Scandal of Service*, 47.

54. Vanier, *Becoming Human*, 21.

only did these professionals assist L'Arche with discerning and understanding the meaningfulness hidden within her state of chaos but also Claudia's need for stability and the security of a structured day.[55] In fact, psychiatrists, psychologists, and assistants played an indispensable role in assisting both Claudia and L'Arche with the more practical aspects of caring for Claudia. Accordingly, "understanding," according to Vanier, "takes time and a great deal of attention, as well as wisdom and help from professionals, in order to learn how to interpret their cries and their body language which reveal the desires and needs they cannot name."[56] What is being implied here is that the place and role of professionals (psychology and psychiatry) in Claudia's case and in L'Arche emanates from an ethos of caring constituted by timefulness, attentiveness, discernment, and listening. In other words, professional competency, while extremely significant within L'Arche, is based on relationship and personal presence and care.[57] Moreover, the more technical aspects of caring within L'Arche, especially in Claudia's case, do not supersede the characteristic spirit that underlies and gives definite form to a way of caring involving humanly sensitive care, costly resources (such as people) and time (such as patience).[58] In this regard, care within L'Arche protects persons like Claudia from the depersonalizing effect(s) of "concomitant professionalizing and specialization of care" in which persons are reduced to the characteristic features of their disability and/or become equivalent to a technical problem to be managed efficiently.[59]

Less than one year after the inception of L'Arche (June 17, 1965) Vanier expresses in a letter to friends L'Arche's desire to make full use of what he would later describe as professional accompaniment. He writes, "L'Arche, while taking its inspiration directly from the Gospels, wants to make full use of psychiatry

55. Ibid., 21, 24.

56. Ibid., 24.

57. Vanier, *An Ark for the Poor*, 120–21.

58. Reynolds, *Vulnerable Communion*, 91. See Vanier, *Our Journey Together*, 19, 22, 43–47.

59. Ibid.

and medicine . . . To remain simple and open to Providence, to the inspirations of the Holy Spirit and to the teachings of Christ and, at the same time, to adapt to the methods of . . . professionals can often be difficult. It is our duty to find a healthy balance between the two."[60] A few years later (November 5, 1968) Vanier would reflect on the ways in which the accompaniment of professionals, specifically psychiatrists, had taken shape in L'Arche. Vanier writes, "Dr. Franko, our new psychiatrist, gave us much of his time and helped us to better understand our role on the psychological level."[61] In the light of Vanier's understanding of "accompaniment" as a way of "being alongside people as a companion and friend in order to help them grow in freedom and in the spirit of the community," involving *cum pane*—"eating bread together, which signifies a bond of friendship, a covenant," these personal accounts on the place and role of psychological/psychiatric accompaniment evidence how professional forms of caring within L'Arche emanate from an ethos of care constituted by timefulness, attentiveness, discernment, and listening.[62]

Accordingly, it is vital to note that Vanier does not identify Claudia's disability or her then prevailing emotional-behavioral symptoms in technical terms beyond that of autism. Neither does he name or allude to Claudia's autism as a disorder. When employing the term "disorder" in relation to Claudia, Vanier contextually situates it in relation to the chaos, madness, inner pain, and anguish stemming from the lived experience of having been isolated and marginalized her entire life rather than in terms of and/or relation to the symptomatic emotional and behavioral conditions associated with autism. Rather than restricting his view of Claudia

60. Vanier, *Our Life Together*, 19. It is widely known that from its inception the roles of medical, psychiatric, and physiological care provision have always had a significant place within L'Arche. See Vanier, *An Ark for the Poor*, 120–21; Edmonds, *A Theological Diagnosis*, 188–89. Also, it is worth mentioning that there is an emerging discourse on the L'Arche communities that not only includes responses from theology but also the sciences. See Reinders, *The Paradox of Disability*, 25–100.

61. Ibid., 44.

62. Vanier, *Community and Growth*, 249–51.

to technical diagnosis, Vanier reads Claudia in the light of her true humanity, that is, in a way that acknowledges the existence of her personhood and as one who possess the right to find her place and to live as fully human as possible.[63] Like Evelyn, who constantly banged her head against floors; Robert, who would often beg others to cut off his genitals; Luke, who aimlessly ran round and round; George, who always seemed tense; Mark, who genuinely believed he was possessed by the devil; Carol, who was deemed a crazy idiot since early childhood; Eric, who was blind, deaf, severely brain-damaged; and the many other persons he has shared life with; Claudia, according to Vanier, is a *person* who carries with her experiences of physical and mental disabilities, not an autistic person. Moreover, Claudia's behaviors are identified in relation to her lived experience of isolation, abandonment, and anguish, or more precisely, "the profound wounding of her heart," which, according to Vanier, is the source of her behavior, regardless of how aggressive, oppositional, depressive, and/or autistic she may seem.[64] Claudia suffered from the image she had been given of her false self, not "the mental condition, present from early childhood, characterized by great difficulty in communicating and forming relationships with other people and/or in using language and abstract concepts; a mental condition in which fantasy dominates over reality, as a symptom of schizophrenia and other disorders."[65] As we will see Vanier does not conflate or collapse the distinction between "persons" and their experience of living with disabilities.[66] Claudia's integration into L'Arche was not for the purpose of determining her diagnosis—what she had—but rather for helping her see herself from the perspective of the person she is. To do otherwise would have had profound implications on the ways in which "health" and "care" were understood, measured, and

63. Vanier, *Man and Woman God Made Them*, 1.

64. Ibid., 12.

65. *Oxford English Dictionary*, 2nd ed., s.v. "Autism."

66. Here I am in conversation with Reynolds on denigrating and trivializing views of persons with disability. See Reynolds, *Vulnerable Communion*, 37–42.

rendered. Seeing Claudia's autism as a disorder could have given rise to a whole set of generalizations that would have depersonalized and objectified both Claudia and her disability as things to be treated and/or cured. As a result, "caring" would have been equivocated to "curing," and "health" would have been measured on the basis of the elimination of Claudia's physical and/or mental deficiencies.

Clearly Vanier's understanding of health and well-being affects the ways in which L'Arche understands and renders care within their communities. Care is oriented toward human growth. "At the basis of all human growth there must be self-esteem, a sense of one's deepest value as a person. We need to be seen as *persons*, not as things," writes Vanier.[67] In the light of Vanier's reflections on caring for Claudia, L'Arche exemplifies the type of care Henri Nouwen describes as being with, crying out with, suffering with, feeling with. "Care is compassion. It is claiming the truth that the other is my brother or sister, human, mortal, vulnerable like I am ... To care is to be human."[68] Care in L'Arche involves nurturing and encouraging the growth of others in love and with and by loving others through belonging and being with and present-*for* others. In this regard, care is a way of life. Vanier substantiates this claim in his description of how one of the aims of L'Arche is to transform the broken self-image of someone like Claudia into a positive self-image, from self-hate to self-love. "People like [Claudia] have led me into the need of community and for a simple lifestyle where the essential is to care for one another, to celebrate life, to be open, and to grow more loving and understanding toward neighbors and friends, a lifestyle where we are no longer each for ourselves alone, but together we are a sign of a new way of life," Vanier explains.[69] Fundamentally, caring for others is constitutive of the distinctive way of living in L'Arche; it is a communal affair involving the recip-

67. Vanier, *Finding Peace*, 33.

68. Nouwen, *Bread for the Journey*, 47.

69. Vanier, "What Have People with Learning Disabilities Taught Me?," 22. In view of my use of Vanier's reflections on Claudia, I have substituted Claudia's name in the place of "Eric" in this citation.

rocal exchange of persons moving persons toward becoming fully human. In Claudia's case, the one who is need of moving toward human wholeness paradoxically becomes the central healer in the life of others, specifically Nadine, the community leader in Suyapa, moving her toward a new way of life. Vanier writes, "And so it was that Claudia gradually began to discover that while Nadine was calling forth new life in her, Claudia was also calling forth new life in Nadine."[70] Hence, care underlies and gives definite form to the radical way of life that L'Arche embodies.

Care: a genuine *humanitas*

In what follows, a brief analysis on the specific ways in which Vanier characterizes what is commonly referred to as the "carer-patient" relationship will be given in order to demonstrate how his account describes an ethos of care that revalues interpersonal relational activity between carers, assistants, and professionals and those they care for as well as raises conceptual questions concerning what constitutes "usefulness" of time within caring contexts. The primary purpose of this section is to demonstrate how Vanier's understanding of the carer–patient relationship is inherently humane in nature. At this point it is vital to note that neither Vanier or L'Arche identify its members with technical descriptions such as "patients" and "caring professionals." Instead, its members are identified as "core members" (people with developmental disabilities) and "those who share life with and support them" (assistants). As we will see, the underlying ethos of shared life, being with and present-*for* others within L'Arche not only informs the grammar that rightly names the division of caring roles among its members but also the intention of care provision within L'Arche—personal presence, juxtaposed with professional intervention and goals of improvement.[71] As we will see, Vanier and L'Arche's synthetic ac-

70. Vanier, *Becoming Human*, 28.

71. For a more detailed theological reading of the distinction between "intervention" and "presence" in relation to care as a way of life within L'Arche, see Reinders, *Receiving the Gift of Friendship*, 336–37.

count of care provision provides a practical lens by which we can theologically distinguish what forms of care and treatment are humane from those that depersonalize and objectify persons.[72] Vanier's account of care provides access to raising conceptual questions about the societal impulses that underlie and give shape to society's judgments about care provision, humanity, and the good as well as the cultural assumptions, technologies, and techniques often perceived as holding personhood in place.

In a way paralleling biblical portrayals of salvation that undermine the power and authority of then prevailing conventional and normate cultural assumptions of redemption by way of focusing on the manifestation of divine presence within vulnerable humanity as "a site of relational interdependence," Vanier offers an account of care contextually embedded in communal milieus that calls attention to the power and presence of God concretized in those whom society sees as weak, vulnerable, poor, and of no account.[73] Vanier describes the distinctive nature and features of God's power and presence in relation to Christ's self-disclosure concerning his identification with what is "unseemly and strange"—persons experiencing sickness and persons with disabilities.[74] On this account, God's presence and power is paradoxically revealed, not in autonomy but in and through vulnerability that assumes mutual dependency. At a deeper level, God's ways with humanity makes listening and responsiveness to God and others necessary for faithful exploration of God's will. In the context of caring, listening and remaining responsive to God is

72. On this account, I have chosen to retain the universal language of description of "carer–patient"—at times utilizing a slash with the term "person" as a way to signify the importance of understanding the "patient as person" more than anything else—in order to characterize the relationship and distinctive roles between care providers and those to whom care is given.

73. Here, I am in conversation with Reynolds's understanding on the "strange logic" inherent to Christian witness, "one that gives testimony to a strength that comes through weakness, a wholeness that manifests itself in brokenness, a power that reveals itself through vulnerability." See Reynolds, *Vulnerable Communion*, 19–20.

74. Migliore, *Faith Seeking Understanding*, 52. See Reynolds, *Vulnerable Communion*, 20n17.

concretized via listening and remaining responsive to, being with and present-*for*, welcoming, and sharing our lives with those who are sick and vulnerable.[75]

Throughout the foregoing analyses and chapters we have examined the ways in which being present-*for* another, in relation to Vanier's understanding of care, involves the selfless gift of one's whole presence for the other's well-being in which the carer lives out his/her fidelity to the concrete reality that the other, namely the sick, lays claim to their being. In so doing, emphasis has been placed on how Vanier's christological move in which he situates the presence of Christ at the center of all caring operations not only calls attention to the ways in which caring for the sick is fundamentally caring for Christ but also protects against technical, impersonal, and pretentious forms of carelessness, affects one's consciousness of the other's personhood and presence, cultivates sincere love, respect, and attentive service for the other—all of which are reciprocal in nature—and makes provision for forms of care that are rendered in honor, fear, and the name of God. For these reasons, the whole nature and scope of caring within L'Arche, as characterized throughout Vanier's writings, originates from a Christocentric perspective that not only forms one's perception of Christ's presence in the other but also one's perception of the value of caring for the other taking into consideration persons welfare and humanity; and thus, preempting forms of care in which pretense, deceit, and self-projection emerge.

We will now turn our attention to more detailed ways in which listening and responsivity not only underlies and influences certain gestures of caring within Vanier's account of care but also foil forms of care to which self-projection, control, and possessive love belong. As a whole, Vanier's account of care refuses the conventional cultural assumptions concerning what provisions are necessary for caring for others. Instead of seeing care from a technical/medical perspective in which caring is perceived in terms of "what" requires prognosis, treatment, and cure (medical/

---

75. Here, I am not suggesting that being sick is equivalent to having a disability.

therapeutic script) and/or "what" needs fixing (technological script), Vanier reads care through a wholly different lens, one that fundamentally revalues the question of care. That is to say, Vanier calls forth different questions: What does it mean to care? In what ways does caring become a conduit for listening and remaining responsive to God, primarily, and others? Care, according to Vanier, appears as a way of life in which caring for others becomes a means for faithful exploration of God's will. Moreover, caring becomes a context in which all time, space, and opportunity is rendered for both the carer and one cared for to be and become fully human. For these reasons, care and caring, for Vanier, do not originate from a place of calculating efficient techniques and solutions that can be applied to those whom treatment, prognosis, and curing is due. What is being implied here is that care, according to Vanier, is not reduced to an exclusive domain of caring activity, that is "doing" things for others. But, it is important to note that I am not suggesting Vanier denies the place and role of caring activity altogether. In fact, the gestures of care are visibly expressed through caring activities, "doing," within L'Arche. But the doing emanates from an ethos of care that inherently is shaped in and by way of the practice of being with and present-*for* others. Therefore, care as way of life gives definite shape to a caring in which *being* with and present-*for* others is oriented toward persons, primarily, and their health instead of sickness and/or vulnerability. In this regard, care as way of life (being) and caring (being as activity) correspond to Vanier's account of how being human is becoming human.

Vanier characterizes an account of care that calls into question contemporary forms of healthcare in which the patient/person plays a notional and/or nominal role at best. His accounts involve an economy built upon human exchange that is reciprocal in nature. Instead of focusing on associative symptoms or conditions of disability and impairment, Vanier situates persons at the center of all caring activity; a strategic move that has important implications for the carer–patient/person relationship, the delivery of care, and "what" is delivered via care provision. Vanier characterizes carers, assistants, and professionals in L'Arche as persons who enter into a committed relationship with persons with disabilities. This commitment is described as "true friendship" in which everything is oriented by this concern for the other person.[76] As we have seen, this type of friendship supposes sharing life together; a mutual belonging constituted by meaningful, authentic, and respectful relationships.[77] "Consideration," "attention," "patience," "commitment," "friendship," and "belonging" all convey modes of creaturely existence involving an indefinite continued progress of interpersonal relational activity unrestricted by the limits of time. What is being implied here is that these characterizations of the carer–patient/person relationship give name to an ethos of care that revalues the usefulness of time within caring context. For instance, "patience" and "consideration" convey an indefinite measure of time for caring rather than a limit and/or restriction of time allotted to each patient/person—a phenomenon occurring within managed health care models in which incentives to restrain costs, deny certain forms of treatment, limit caring, and ensure cost-effective medicine drive and determine the value of care while at the same time restrain and injure the physician–patient relationship.[78] Additionally, "commitment," "friendship," and "belonging" give name to a caring relationship entailing the actual presence of persons who possess shared values, inclusive behaviors, and communitarian goals. In this regard, the "carer–patient" relationship, or more precisely, "the core member and assistant" relationship in L'Arche is not limited to the context or circumstances of caring. It extends beyond the boundaries of the infirmary, counseling session, and/or foyer. These type of relationships preempt depersonalizing forms of care that objectify and degrade persons to an abstract or static status as well as the temptation to conflate the distinction between sick persons and their constraints; collapsing gestures that often result in modes of caring in which the management of behaviors and/or the limits externally caused by sickness

76. Vanier, *Made for Happiness*, 54–75, esp. 66.

77. Vanier, "What Have People with Learning Disabilities Taught Me?," 20–21. See Vanier, *Made for Happiness*, 54.

78. Evans, *Redeeming Marketplace Medicine*, 14.

underlie, influence, and drive care. In addition, these relationships simultaneously provide access for ways of caring in which carers can affirm persons humanity, dignity, and value by way of belonging and being with and present-*for* others. On this account, Vanier's understanding of the carer-patient relationship is inherently humane in nature.

Another feature within Vanier's account of care is the notion of service. Vanier writes, "We attain human maturity as we live relationships more deeply and become open to others and ready to serve them."[79] He continues, "Community life in L'Arche is founded on heart-to-heart relationships and the joy of recognizing our common humanity. We are discovering that relationship begins with an attitude of receptivity and by welcoming others, listening to them, and trusting them."[80] Vanier sees care as service from the perspective of a way of life involving a posture of humble service constituted by listening and remaining responsive to others. In the context of caring service, the carer who serves gives their whole energy, devotion, and self for the other without seeking any advantage from the benefit and/or production of caring. In other words, caring as a service is something other than the contractual service involving the economic exchange of goods and products for payment.

When theologically viewed through a service lens care is inherent to Christian witness. The carer concretizes his or her love for Christ by way of caring for (serving) persons who are sick and persons with disabilities. In *Befriending the Stranger* Vanier describes the ways in which caring for others in L'Arche in which persons live and journey together, men and women with disabilities and those who feel called to share their lives with them through the pains and joys of community life not only epitomizes "a way of being" that is rooted in Christ-like humility and service but also exemplifies the vision of God in which [Jesus] "moves down the social ladder to take the lowest place in order to "be

79. Vanier, *The Scandal of Service*, 3.
80. Ibid., 4

with" the weak and the broken."[81] Hence, an ethos of service and humility underlies and gives definite shape to caring in L'Arche. While making this point more clear Vanier explicitly employs the term *serve* in contextual relation to the aim(s) of L'Arche: "Persons attain maturity as they live relationships more deeply and become open to others and ready to *serve* them."[82] Through "simplicity and humility" Jesus "embraces the lost and broken, and with them creates communities of hope, communities of the Kingdom."[83] In this regard, L'Arche concretizes the divine embrace of the lost and broken in contemporary society by way of being with and present-*for* persons with disabilities. On this account, Vanier theologically characterizes the carer as a Christ-type, a servant, who visibly expresses her attentive listening and loving responsiveness to God by way of serving others in care. At a deeper level this characterization conveys the ways in which caring is primarily a service to persons in which the carer concretizes their listening and responsiveness to God by means of rendering all necessary time, space, and opportunity, as well as one's self for the other without seeking to benefit one's own self-productivity and/or performance.

Within the foregoing analysis on Vanier's reflections on Claudia I placed emphasis on how Claudia's medical needs were not the primary cause and/or impulse underlying and/or giving shape to the care she received in L'Arch. Because Claudia's wholeness and health were not determined in relation to the successful treatment of her autism, curing her blindness, and/or the effective implementation of modifying behaviors, emotions, and/or a daily schedule, I explained how health, according to Vanier, is something other than curing or the state of being free from physical, mental, emotional, and psychological impairment, illness or injury. On this account, caring is not equivocated or reductively defined in terms of relieving or eliminating symptoms and conditions often associated with a disease, injury, or impairment. Neither is health measured on the basis of the management or exclusion of Claudia's

81. Vanier, *Befriending the Stranger*, 41.
82. Vanier, *The Scandal of Service*, 3. Italics mine.
83. Ibid.

physical and mental deficiencies. Moreover, this particular account of care found within Vanier's writings is paradigmatic of the whole economy of care within L'Arche; an economy of care undergirded, informed, and given definite shape by a genuine *humanitas* that is best characterized as being present-*for* the other, which involves being and belonging with the other.

Care and Community as Faithful Exploration

In the light of the foregoing analyses, Vanier sees listening and remaining responsive to God and others not as supplemental gestures of caring but rather as integral constituents of the distinctive nature underlying and giving definite form to the characteristic spirit of care within community. In view of all the preceding theological investigations on the ways in which "caring" is concretized within L'Arche, it is my contention that listening and responsivity constitute the characteristic nature and scope of care within Vanier's accounts as a whole. Vanier's communal account of caring offers a vision of the Christian moral life concretized in a narration of care as a way of life that is given shape in listening and remaining responsive to the presence of God and others. Moreover, caring within L'Arche is not based on an ideal. While readers may interpret certain characteristics and gestures of caring within Vanier's writings and L'Arche as moral proscriptions and/or prescriptions it is important to note that Vanier never legislates an exhaustive list of ethical imperatives concerning how to and/or how not to care for persons with disabilities. Vanier never says, "These are the ways in which you are to care for the sick." Nor does he set in motion a particular law or structured legislation for caring *for* others within L'Arche communities. Hence, care as a way of life within L'Arche is not about trying to implement the ideal amount and/or types of caring gestures; rather, it is about learning to care for others in ways that visibly express one's fidelity to the concrete reality that other lays claim to another's' being.[84] This phenomenon supposes a faithful exploration of God's will in which persons actively enter into a caring relationship, or more precisely, a way of life involving a life-long process of learning how to listen and remain responsive to others. What is being implied here is that in caring for others one encounters God. The other offers a way in which the carer can listen and remain responsive to God in the world, others, and one's "true self." Through caring for the other carers visibly manifest their responsiveness to God through remaining present-*for* the other. Because his communal account places value on the ways in which God's activity and presence within the story of creaturely existence plays a role in forming the way the intricacies of caring are enacted, Vanier offers a theological account of care in which Christ's presence gives shape to the way of caring for others as well as an account of faith taking shape through a shared way of living and encountering God, primarily, and others. As we have seen, Vanier answers the existential question, "How does one listen and remain responsive to the activity and presence of God in this life?" by way of concretizing Christ's presence among those who are sick, poor, and vulnerable as a way to cultivate an ethos of belonging and being present-*for* the other.

The particularity of Christ's claim on our lives, for Vanier, is concretized within the quotidian fabric of creaturely life, particularly with reference to the claims that God's Word, creation, and others lay on our lives. However, life, according to Vanier, is not an occasion for applying moral principles but rather for listening and remaining responsive to the One who lays claim on the moral life of self-conscious creatures. For this reason, Vanier clarifies the discussion of what is universal within Christian ethics by way of drawing attention to the central claim of the gospel—that is to say, Christ is Lord of all creation. On this account, the task of ethics is situated where peoples' lives are, and in the context of Christian

---

84. A common response to Jean Vanier and L'Arche communities is that Vanier's understanding of "community" is not about trying to live a shared ideal; rather it is about learning the truth about oneself and others. See Reinders, *The Paradox of Disability*, 6.

community in particular, in which one's responsiveness to Christ's claim on our creaturely existence is visibly expressed in listening and remaining responsive to the constant form of God's presence in the world, or more precisely, "God's ways *with* humanity." Moreover, becoming conscious of this dynamic of faith involves faithful exploration of God's presence, especially in connection with God's existential relation to us mediated in and through God's Word, creation, and others as they interrelate in Christ. As we have seen, God's existential relation to humanity, according to Vanier, is fundamentally discovered by way of others in communion, life together.

Foundational for Vanier is the centrality of the Word of God. Christ is the fundamental reality that underlies and gives definite form to community as a way of life as well as the attitudes that inform living within community. Throughout his writings, Vanier situates the presence and activity of Christ in relation to those whom Christ identifies with in the gospels—the poor, vulnerable, and weak. In L'Arche, those whom society marginalize and discard to a place of no account possess a central role and place within the community. In L'Arche, the weak, vulnerable, and poor are persons through whom God's presence is revealed.[85] Hence, remaining responsive to the weak, vulnerable, and poor concretizes one's faithful exploration of listening and remaining responsive to the presence of Christ. At this point it is important to note that this does not mean Vanier sees Christ's presence "only" in persons who are weak and vulnerable. Nor does L'Arche and Vanier seek to establish or legislate a rule for determining if persons actually represent Christ's presence. The point I am making is that Christ, though present in each person, is especially present in the weakest, those at the center of L'Arche. Moreover, persons with disabilities and those who are weak and sick are the least of these in the light of a society that privileges autonomy, power, and prestige. Since they are considered the least of these, they render Christ present. In other words, their poverty, the very conditions whereof they are considered as being the least of these, "is a predisposition to

85. Vanier, *An Ark for the Poor*, 150.

receive the graces of love that Jesus has promised to them" and the honor of being a conduit for visibly manifesting the characteristic spirit, activity, and presence of Christ within the story of human existence (Matt 25).[86] Therefore, listening and remaining responsive to the presence and activity of God within L'Arche is not so much to try to identify with Christ, imitating him and acting in ways corresponding to one's imagining how Christ would act if he were in our situation. No, the goal of L'Arche is to acknowledge those with whom Christ has chosen to identify. On this account, the integral constituent that underlies and gives definite form to these communities is the presence of the Christ. Because Christ, "is the primary and basic reality that underlies and gives shape to all community life, then it might be said emphatically that the essential and basic attitude of persons living in communities [like L'Arche] must be one of listening and responsiveness."[87] Necessarily, anything or person that diverts, distracts, or disturbs the communal and individual attitudes of listening and responsiveness to God and others, breaks down community, and necessarily prevents both one's self and others from being and becoming fully human.

Within this account, listening and remaining responsive to God's ways within human existence are visibly expressed not through sanctioned roles instituted by Vanier or as required additions that support other primary gestures of love, structures, tasks, and attitudinal responses, but rather as integral constituents of the characteristic spirit of their communal accounts exemplified via faithful exploration of God's ways with humanity in the course of life. For this reason, it is my contention that Vanier's understanding of community offers a holistic vision of the Christian moral life expressed visibly in a narration of community as a way of life in which faithful exploration of the presence of God within the course of creaturely life is made possible in and through listening and remaining responsive to the constant form and reality of God's

86. Vanier, *Our Life Together,* 11.

87. Hanron, "Can We Dialogue with Today's World on Community?," 363.

active Word, will, and presence within creation. Therefore, "true community begins with a listening heart."[88]

Since Vanier's communal account presupposes that God, for Vanier, is presently active within the quotidian fabric of creaturely life, an implication comes to the fore; namely, that the unique nature of the ethical form of self-conscious creaturely life is characterized by a distinct form of listening and responsiveness. The constant form of God's presence and activity within the world to which all creaturely existence is called to faithfully explore within the course of a life in which circumstances obtain, according to Vanier, is linked to the social context of persons who are vulnerable, poor, and profoundly weak—those whom Christ identifies with in the Gospels. Vanier describes concrete circumstances concerning the ways in which self-conscious creatures can listen and remain responsive to the constant form of God's presence—the constant pneumatological reality in the church and presence of Christ in the world—in experience. In so doing, Vanier revalues the notion of ethics as faith's listening and remaining responsive to the conduits of divine presence in the church and world. For this reason, becoming conscious of this dynamic of faith involves faithful exploration of life within and under Christ's particular claim on creaturely life concretized in others interrelated in Christ. Hence, Vanier's communal account is grounded in the sobriety of a naked realism involving listening and responsiveness to God in the present moment. It is precisely in the present encounter that persons in L'Arche, and within the world, in general, participate in faithful exploration in listening and remaining responsive to God's Word, will, presence, activity, and ways with humanity.

88. Ibid., 369.

Conclusion

ABIDE IN MY LOVE. Reflecting on these words of Jesus, Vanier writes, "We can't deny that today our lives and those of our society are shot through with absurdity. But when love passes through absurdity, it has the power to transform it into presence. And in this presence we can live . . . Abide with Jesus as he washed the feet of the poor. This is the path he shows us, for the feet of the poor are also the feet of Jesus."[1] For Vanier, a life that reveals true value to oneself and others is a life that inhabits humility, a life characterized by love for and loving service to those who are excluded and socially insignificant.[2] For more than five decades Vanier and L'Arche have discovered and continue to discover what it means to welcome others through listening and remaining responsive to those whom society ghettoizes as absurd, having little or no sense, use, or purpose. Vanier and L'Arche offer a radical vision of life together in which genuine welcome rests upon a communal commitment to abide in a love that does not hide, a love that is willing to pass through that which society deems absurd. For Vanier and L'Arche, to abide in love entails not hiding ourselves behind the masks of our own making, the false self that attempts to exalt power and possession above presence, but rather to abide in love through and through, allowing love's power to pass through and transform all that might seem or be absurd into presence in which we can live. Following the path of Jesus, Vanier and L'Arche have

1. Jean Vanier, *Signs*, 89.
2. Ibid., 84.

and continue to wash the feet of the poor—those who experience life cognitively, physically, emotionally, and/or socially different from the societal majority—persons with disabilities. As a result, they have and continue to bear witness to the scandalous reality that the feet of the poor are also the feet of Jesus, revealing to the church and world that those we deem absurd are absolutely necessary. They are necessary not only because they are paradigmatic of God's coming kingdom, "a kingdom where the weakest and the most humble are given the prominent place," but also a presence of God within the world.[3] What is being implied here is that the presence in which we can live is a presence that is made possible by welcoming, listening, and remaining responsive to God whose superabundance is hidden behind his omnipotence in the smallness, weakness, and absurdity of the least powerful among us; to live within this presence is to allow ourselves to be led by them.[4]

To abide in love is to embody a way of life that inhabits humility to welcome others. For it is in welcoming the other that we welcome God's presence within the story of our lives. Welcome as a way of life presupposes that welcome possesses an intrinsic relationship to creaturely worship. How we welcome others visibly expresses the measure of moral fiber of the church's being, act, and understanding of worship. Jean Vanier's writings and L'Arche visibly express a way of life that is given shape in welcoming, listening and remaining responsive to others; others, and especially God. As we have seen, listening underlies, informs, and gives definite shape to community and care as a way of life, making genuine welcome within L'Arche possible. Correspondingly, listening gives shape to welcome as a way of life that entails living out one's fidelity to the commonly held vision that the other lays claim to our being; a way of life characterized in living together, being with and present-*for* others. Read from this perspective, genuine welcome originates in

3. Vanier, *The Scandal of Service*, 32; 50. Commenting on various Gospel accounts such as Matthew 25; Mark 10:14–15; and Luke 9:48, 12:35–37, 14, Vanier writes, "But with Jesus we are all invited to discover how the poor and outcast are a presence of God."

4. Vanier, *Signs*, 86.

a commonly held vision about what constitutes humanity, community, communion, and care; humanity is shared, community is a way of life in which faithful listening to others makes welcome possible, and communion is vital for humanity.

On the whole, welcome is integral to if not representative of the whole characteristic ethos and way of life within L'Arche. Vanier and L'Arche offer a radical vision of the ways in which the specificity of Christ's claim on one's self is concretized within the story of our lives in and through welcoming the other. To abide in love is to welcome others.

Bibliography

Aristotle. *Nicomachean Ethics*. Edited by J. Rackham. Cambridge, MA: Loeb Classical Library, 1934.

Balthasar, Hans Urs von. *The Theology of Henri de Lubac: An Overview*. San Francisco: Communio, 1991.

Böckmann, Aquinata. *Growing in Mutual Service and Love Around the Monastic Table*. Collegeville, MN: Liturgical, 2009.

Boersma, Hans. "Sacramental Ontology: Nature and the Supernatural in the Ecclesiology of Henri de Lubac." *New Blackfriars* vol. 88, issue 1015 (2007) 242–73.

Bonhoeffer, Dietrich. *Ethics*. New York: Simon & Schuster, 1995.

Brock, Brian. *Christian Ethics in a Technological Age*. Grand Rapids: Eerdmans, 2010.

———. "Theologizing Inclusion: 1 Corinthians 12 and the Politics of the Body of Christ." *The Journal of Religion, Disability & Health* 15.4 (2011) 351–76.

Brock, Brian, and John Swinton, eds. *Disability in the Christian Tradition: A Reader*. Grand Rapids: Eerdmans, 2012.

Brueggemann, Walter. "Counterscript." *Christian Century* 122 (2005) 22–28.

Buber, Martin. *Between Man and Man*. London: Routledge, 1947.

Burrell, David. *Aquinas: God and Action*. London: Routledge and Kegan Paul, 1979.

Cerac, Odile. "The Poor at the Heart of Our Communities." In *The Challenge of L'Arche*, 25–35. London: Darton, Longman & Todd, 1982.

Congar, Yves. *The Wide World My Parish*. Translated by Donald Attwater. London: Darton, Longman & Todd, 1961.

Doyle, Dennis M. "Henri de Lubac and the Roots of Communion Ecclesiology." *Theological Studies* 60 (1990) 226–27.

Dufresne, Jacques. "A Road to Freedom." http://www.jean-vanier.org.en.his_message/a_philosophy/a_road_to_freedom.

———. "Jean Vanier: A Philosophy." http://www.jean-vanier.org/en/his_message/a_philosophy.

Edmonds, Matt. *A Theological Diagnosis: A New Direction on Genetic Therapy, 'Disability' and the Ethics of Healing*. London: Jessica Kingsley, 2011.

Eusebius. *Church History*. Translated by Arthur Cushman McGiffert. In vol. 1 of The Nicene and Post-Nicene Fathers, Series 2, edited by Philip Schaff. 14 vols. Grand Rapids: Eerdmans, 1956.

Evans, Abigail Rian. *Redeeming Marketplace Medicine: A Theology of Health Care*. Cleveland: Pilgrim, 1999.

Ford, David F. "L'Arche and Jesus: What is Theology?" In *Encounter with Mystery: Reflections on L'Arche and Living with Disability*, edited by Frances Young, 77–88. London: Darton, Longman, & Todd, 1997.

Gutiérrez, Gustavo. *A Theology of Liberation: History, Politics, and Salvation*. Translated by Sister Caridad Inda, et al. Maryknoll, NY: Orbis, 1973.

Hall, Katharine Ann. "An Inquiry into the Theology and Practice of Covenantal Living in L'Arche." MA thesis, University of Exeter, 2011.

Hanron, Margaret Mary. "Can We Dialogue with Today's World on Community?" *Cistercian Studies* 15 (1980) 359–69.

Hauerwas, Stanley. *A Community of Character: Toward a Constructive Christian Social Ethic*. Notre Dame, IN: University of Notre Dame Press, 1981.

———. "Community and Diversity: The Tyranny of Normality." In *Critical Reflections on Stanley Hauerwas' Theology of Disability: Disabling Society, Enabling Theology*, edited by John Swinton, 37–43. Binghamptom, NY: Haworth Pastoral, 2004.

———. "Seeing Peace: L'Arche as a Peace Movement." In *The Paradox of Disability: Responses to Jean Vanier and L'Arche Communities from Theology and Sciences*, edited by Hans S. Reinders, 113–26. Cambridge: Eerdmans, 2010.

Hauerwas, Stanley, and Jean Vanier. *Living Gently in a Violent World: The Prophetic Witness of Weakness*. Downers Grove, IL: InterVarsity, 2008.

Havel, Vaclav. "The Power of the Powerless." http://vaclavhavel.cz/showtrans. php?cat=eseje&val=2_aj_eseje.html&typ=HTML.

Holburn, S., and P. M. Vietz. *Person Centered Planning: Research, Practice, and Future Directions*. Baltimore: Paul H. Brookes, 2002.

International Alliance of Patients' Organizations (IAPO) Declaration on Patient-Centered Healthcare." http://www.patientsorganizations.org/showarticle.pl?id=712&n=312.

John Paul II. *Encyclical Letter Sollicitudo Rei Socialis*. Vatican City: Libreria Edetrice Vaticana, 1987.

Kilbane, Jackie, and Tom McLean. "Exploring the history of person centred practice." In *Person Centred Practice for Professionals*, edited by Jeanette Thompson, Jackie Kilbane, and Helen Sanderson, 3–25. Berkshire: Open University Press, 2008.

Kleinman, Arthur. *The Illness Narratives: Suffering, Healing, and the Human Condition*. New York: Basic, 1988.

Komonchak, Joseph A. "Theology and Culture at Mid-Century: The Example of Henri de Lubac." *Theological Studies* 51 (1990) 579–602.

L'Arche International. "Communities of L'Arche." http://www.larche.org/charter-of-the-communities-of-l-arche.en-gb.43.3.content.htm.

———. "L'Arche since its beginnings." http://www.larche.org/l-arche-since-its-beginnings.en-gb.22.10.content.htm.

———. "Our History." http://www.larche.org/discover/ourhistory/.

Lawler, M. G. "Perichoresis: New Theological Wine in An Old Theological Wineskin." *Horizons* 22 (1995) 49.

Luz, Ulrich. "Matthew: a Commentary." *Hermeneia: A Critical & Historical Commentary on the Bible.* Minneapolis: Augsburg Fortress, 2005.

MacIntyre, Alasdair. *After Virtue: a Study in Moral Theory.* 2nd ed. London: Duckworth, 1985.

———. *Whose Justice? Which Rationality?* Notre Dame, IN: University of Notre Dame Press, 1988.

McGrath, Alister. *Christian Theology: An Introduction.* Oxford: Wiley-Blackwell, 2011.

Migliore, Daniel L. *Faith Seeking Understanding: An Introduction to Christian Theology.* Grand Rapids: Eerdmans, 1991.

Milbank, John. *The Suspended Middle: Henri de Lubac and the Debate Concerning the Supernatural.* Grand Rapids: Eerdmans, 2005.

Nietzsche, Friedrich. *The Twilight of the Idols and The Anti-Christ: or How to Philosophize with a Hammer.* Edited by Michael Tanner. London: Penguin Classics, 1990.

Nouwen, Henri. *Bread for the Journey.* New York: HarperOne, 1997.

Oden, Amy G. *And You Welcomed Me: A Sourcebook on Hospitality in Early Christianity.* Nashville: Abingdon, 2001.

O'Keefe, Mark. "The Unity of Christian Morality and Spirituality: A Benedictine Witness." *American Benedictine Review* 48.1 (1997) 3–18.

O'Regan, John. "Listening." *The Furrow,* vol. 25, no. 10 (1974) 556–60.

Orr, William F., and James Arthur Walther. "1 Corinthians." In *The Anchor Bible.* New York: Doubleday, 1976.

Paul VI. *Gaudium et Spes: Pastoral Constitution on the Church in the Modern World.* Washington: United States Catholic Conference, 1965.

Peck, Scott. *People of the Lie.* New York: Simon and Schuster, 1993.

———. *The Road Less Traveled.* New York: Simon and Schuster, 1978.

Pope Paul VI. *Decree on the Adaptation and Renewal of Religious Life: Perfectae Caritatis.* Vatican II: October 28, 1965.

Reinders, Hans S. "Being with the Disabled: Jean Vanier's Theological Realism." In *Disability in the Christian Tradition,* edited by Brian Brock and John Swinton, 467–511. Cambridge: Eerdmans, 2012.

———. *The Paradox of Disability: Responses to Jean Vanier and L'Arche Communities from Theology and Sciences.* Cambridge: Eerdmans, 2010.

———. *Receiving the Gift of Friendship: Profound Disability, Theological Anthropology, and Ethics.* Grand Rapids: Eerdmans, 2008.

Reinders, Hans, and John Swinton. "Frontiers in Theology and Disability." Presentation, Summer Institute on Theology and Disability. Atlanta, May 26, 2015.

Reynolds, Thomas E. *Vulnerable Communion: A Theology of Disability and Hospitality.* Grand Rapids: Brazos, 2008.

Roberts, Augustine. *Centered on Christ: A Guide to Monastic Profession.* Kalamazoo, MI: Cistercian, 2005.

Rowland, Tracey. *Culture and the Thomist Tradition after Vatican II.* London: Routledge, 2003.

Salenson, Christian. *L'Arche: A Unique and Multiple Spirituality.* Trosly, France: L'Arche en France, 2009.

Sanderson, H. "PCP: Key Features and Approaches." http://www.helensander sonassociates.co.uk/PDFs/PCP%20Key%20Features%20and%20Styles. pdf.

Sartre, Jean-Paul. *No Exit (Huis Clos).* New York: Vintage International, 1989.

Schuman, James. *The Body of Compassion: Ethics, Medicine, and the Church.* Eugene, OR: Wipf and Stock, 1999.

Sigerist, Henry. *The Great Doctors: A Biographic History of Medicine.* Garden City, NY: Doubleday, 1958.

Spink, Kathryn. *The Miracle, the Message, the Story: Jean Vanier and L'Arche.* London: Darton, Longman, & Todd, 2006.

Studzinski, Raymond. *Reading to Live: The Evolving Practice of Lectio Divina.* Collegeville, MN: Liturgical, 2009.

Swinton, John. *From Bedlam to Shalom: Towards a Practical Theology of Human Nature, Interpersonal Relationships, and Mental Health Care.* New York: Peter Lang, 2000.

———. "Beyond Kindness: The Place of Compassion in a Forensic Mental Health Setting." *Health and Social Care Chaplaincy* 1.1 (2013) 11–21.

———. *Spirituality and Mental Health Care: Rediscovering A 'Forgotten' Dimension.* London: Jessica Kingsley, 2001.

———. *Resurrecting the Person: Friendship and the Care of People with Mental Health Problems.* Nashville: Abingdon, 2000.

Swinton, John, and Hans Reinders. "Frontiers in Theology and Disability." Presentation at the Institute on Theology and Disability, Atlanta, May 26, 2015.

Taylor, Charles. *Sources of the Self: The Making of the Modern Identity.* Cambridge, MA: Harvard University Press, 1989.

Thompson, Rosemary Garland. *Extraordinary Bodies: Figuring Phsyical Disability in American Culture and Literature.* New York: Columbia University Press, 1997.

Young, Frances. *Encounter with Mystery: Reflections on L'Arche and Living with Disability.* London: Darton, Longman, & Todd, 1997.

Vanier, Jean. *An Ark for the Poor: The Story of L'Arche.* Toronto: Novalis, 1995.

———. *Becoming Human.* London: Darton, Longman, & Todd, 1999.

———. *Befriending the Stranger.* London: Darton, Longman, & Todd, 2005.

———. *Be Still and Listen.* Ontario: Daybreak, 1975.

———. *The Broken Body.* London: Darton, Longman, & Todd, 1988.

———. *The Challenge of L'Arche.* London: Darton, Longman & Todd, 1982.

―――. *Community and Growth*. London: Darton, Longman, & Todd, 2007.

―――. *Drawn into the Mystery of Jesus through the Gospel of John*. London: Darton, Longman, & Todd, 2004.

―――. *Encountering 'the Other.'* Dublin, Ireland: Veritas, 2005.

―――. *Eruption to Hope*. Toronto: Griffin House, 1971.

―――. *Finding Peace*. London: Continuum, 2003.

―――. "The Fragility of L'Arche and the Friendship of God." In *Living Gently in a Violent World: The Prophetic Witness of Weakness*, edited by John Swinton, 21–41. Downers Grove, IL: InterVarsity, 2008.

―――. *From Brokenness to Community*. Mahwah, NJ: Paulist, 1992.

―――. *Happiness: A Guide to a Good Life, Aristotle for the New Century*. New York: Arcade, 2002.

―――. *Jesus, The Gift of Love*. NY: Crossroad, 2011.

―――. "L'Arche—A Place of Communion and Pain." In *Encounter with Mystery: Reflections on L'Arche and Living with Disability*, edited by Frances Young, 3–17. London: Darton, Longman, & Todd, 1997.

―――. *Living Gently in a Violent World: The Prophetic Witness of Weakness*. Edited by John Swinton. Downers Grove, IL: InterVarsity, 2008.

―――. *Made for Happiness: Discovering the Meaning of Life with Aristotle*. London: Darton, Longman, & Todd, 2001.

―――. *Man and Woman God Made Them*. London: Darton, Longman, & Todd, 2007.

―――. "A man becoming human." https://web.archive.org/web/20120527085451/http://www.jean-vanier.org/l-arche-giving-life.en-gb.97.0.news.htm.

―――. *Our Journey Home: Rediscovering a Common Humanity beyond Our Differences*. London: Hodder & Stoughton, 1997.

―――. *Our Life Together: A Memoir in Letters*. London: Darton, Longman, & Todd, 2008.

―――. "Prepared Remarks." Templeton Prize Ceremony at St. Martin-in-the-Fields, London, May 18, 2015.

―――. *The Scandal of Service: Jesus Washes Our Feet*. Darton, Longman & Todd, 1996.

―――. *Signs: Seven Words of Hope*. New York: Paulist Press, 2013.

―――. "The Transforming Power of People with Disabilities." In *The Vocation of Theology Today: A Festschrift for David Ford*, edited by Tom Greggs et al., 345–58. Eugene, OR: Cascade, 2013.

―――. "The Vision of Jesus." In *Living Gently in a Violent World: The Prophetic Witness of Weakness*, edited by John Swinton, 59–75. Downers Grove, IL: InterVarsity, 2008.

―――. "What Have People with Learning Disabilities Taught Me?" In *The Paradox of Disability: Responses to Jean Vanier and L'Arche Communities from Theology and Sciences*, edited by Hans S. Reinders, 19–24. Cambridge: Eerdmans, 2010.

Wannenwetsch, Bernd. "'Take Heed What Ye Hear': Listening as a Moral, Transcendental and Sacramental Act." *Journal of the Royal Musical Association*, Vol. 135: S1 (2010) 91–102.

Whitney-Brown, Carolyn. *Jean Vanier: Essential Writings*. Maryknoll, NY: Orbis, 2008.

Wolterstorff, Nicholas. "Living Within a Text." In *Faith and Narrative*, edited by Keith E. Yandell, 202–13. Oxford: Oxford University Press, 2001.

Wynn, Kerry H. "The Normate Hermeneutical and Interpretations of Disability within Yahwistic Narratives." In *The Abled Body: Rethinking Disabilities in Biblical Studies*, edited by Hector Avalos, et al., 91–101. Atlanta: Society of Biblical Literature, 2007.

Yong, Amos. *The Bible, Disability, and the Church: A New Vision of the People of God*. Grand Rapids: Eerdmans, 2011.

Printed in Great Britain
by Amazon